Sunset

ATTRACTING BIRDS

BY THE EDITORS OF SUNSET BOOKS

SUNSET BOOKS · MENLO PARK, CALIFORNIA

BRING ON THE BIRDS

Sunset published its first book about birds—*Introduction to Western Birds*—in 1953. In the decades since then, and even since *Sunset* brought out *An Illustrated Guide to Attracting Birds* in 1990, bird-watching and bird-feeding have increased enormously in popularity across North America.

Whereas bird-feeding supplies were once pretty much the province of feed and hardware stores, today you're likely to find a store specializing in them in just about any urban area across the country. If not—turn to the Internet or leaf through a birding magazine to find myriad suppliers of paraphernalia that's strictly for the birds.

Why this explosion of interest? Perhaps it's the natural tendency to cherish our wild heritage as our ties to it become more tenuous. Or perhaps it's the desire to create sanctuaries for ourselves in our own backyards. The sound of birdsong, the splash of wings in a garden pond—these offer a joyous and accessible antidote to today's hectic pace. Birds bring beauty, mystery, and magic into our lives.

Turning your garden into a sanctuary for birds, as well as for you, doesn't need to be complicated. This book is a primer on each aspect of the process, from planning and planting your "birdscape" to feeding and housing the birds that visit it. We introduce you to the basics of bird identification—and provide detailed profiles of many birds you're likely to see in your yard.

In putting together this new edition, we were once again struck by the generosity of birders in sharing their specialized knowledge. A debt of gratitude is owed to many individuals and organizations who have contributed to the team effort of producing *Sunset*'s books about birds over the years. For this edition, we especially thank the National Geographic Society; Joanie Smith of Wild Bird Center in Walnut Creek, California; and Richard Clarke of Birdhouses by Richard Clarke in Estacada, Oregon.

SUNSET BOOKS

Vice President and General Manager: Richard A. Smeby
Editorial Director: Bob Doyle
Production Director: Lory Day
Art Director: Vasken Guiragossian

Staff for this book:
Book Editor: Phyllis Elving
Research and Text: Daniel P. Murphy, Kit and George Harrison,
    Philip Edinger, Scott Atkinson
Additional Text: Rosemary McCreary
Managing Editor: Susan Bryant Caron
Sunset Books Senior Editor, Gardening: Suzanne Normand Eyre
Copy Editor: Jan deProsse, Eagle Eye Editorial Services
Photo Researcher: Tishana Peebles
Production Coordinator: Patricia S. Williams
Special Contributors: Jean Warboy, Barbara Brown, Lisa Anderson
Proofreader: Bridget Biscotti Bradley

Art Director: Alice Rogers
Additional Page Layouts: Elisa Tanaka
Illustrators: Lois Lovejoy, Bill Oetinger, Erin O'Toole, Elayne Sears,
    Jenny Speckels
Computer Production: Joan Olson, Linda M. Bouchard

Cover: American goldfinches are attracted to a seed feeder amid the rosy blooms of a flowering dogwood (*Cornus florida* 'Rubra'). Photography by Harry Haralambou. Border photograph by Claire Curran.

10 9 8 7 6 5 4 3 2
First printing January 2000
Copyright © 2000 Sunset Books Inc., Menlo Park, CA 94025. Second edition.
All rights reserved, including the right of reproduction in whole or in part in any form. Library of Congress Catalog Card Number: 99-66029. ISBN 0-376-03093-3. For additional copies of *Attracting Birds* or any other *Sunset* book, call 1-800-526-5111 or visit our website: www.sunsetbooks.com.

Printed in the United States

Contents

Look up: Like windblown leaves, a hundred pine siskins swirl into a treetop. Peer into a tangled thicket of roses through thorny branches and glimpse a nestful of blue-green catbird eggs. Watch

BIRDS IN YOUR
GARDEN

bandit-masked cedar waxwings splashing in a birdbath, and see a flicker flashing red brushstrokes as it wings away toward its forest home.

Such scenes, as extraordinary as they are common-place, make a backyard birder's heart beat faster—and can quickly turn a casual observer into an avian enthusiast. Birds give us entrée into the wild world in a way that's unique in our increasingly tame landscapes. No wonder that one-third of the U.S. population feeds or watches birds at least occasionally.

Birds put on a show that's unsurpassed for sweet oper-atics and aerial ballet. It's free, it's open-air, and it's conve-nient; you can observe birds in endlessly entertaining activity virtually anytime and everywhere. And best of all, you can bring the performance right into your own backyard. It sim-ply requires an understanding of what birds need and what you can do to meet those needs in your garden.

Amid purple coneflowers, golden rudbeckias, and rosy Joe Pye weed *(Eupatorium),* a rustic birdfeeder expands this garden's attractions for a blue jay (left) and a black-capped chickadee.

WELCOMING WILD BIRDS

Planning a garden to welcome birds goes beyond simply setting out a feeder and hoping that the birds will notice. It starts with observing which birds have already taken up residence in your neighborhood, or pass through seasonally. Each kind of bird has particular preferences for food and shelter, and learning these is the first step toward inviting the birds into your yard.

A fledgling robin finds a convenient garden perch.

Any bird's survival needs are simple, if not always easily met. Happily, a thoughtfully planned garden can provide all of them. No single landscape will satisfy all needs for all the species of birds that may visit, but you can certainly encourage many different birds to stop by—and stay.

Even in the desert, birds will find your garden if it's planned with them in mind. Here, Arizona mesquite trees form a canopy over a border that includes yellow brittle bush, purple *Dalea frutescens,* bamboo muhly grass, and red salvia. DESIGN: Jeffrey Trent.

A CHANGING WORLD

Since civilization began to spread across the continent a couple of centuries ago, the habitats of North American birds have changed radically. Birds were forced to adjust to the dramatic reshaping of their world as forests were cut down, mountains

BOUNTY FOR BIRDS
Late summer vegetation along a rural western roadside feeds several species: robins, spotted towhees, and a thrasher harvesting wild blackberries; bushtits sampling white yarrow seeds; and a goldfinch dining on a teasel. On the far left is a meadowlark, and in the distance barn swallows swoop toward home.

reshaped, prairies plowed, marshes and ponds drained, and arid regions turned green by irrigation.

Some birds responded over the years by restricting themselves to their ever-shrinking original habitats. The result has been the extinction of some species, like the ivory-billed woodpecker, and decreased numbers of many other species.

Other species have adapted resourcefully, increasing their ranges to cultivated fields, islands of trees, or the varied garden habitats provided in towns, suburbs, and even cities. Mockingbirds, cardinals, and house finches, among others, have actually widened their ranges in this way. The "cliff" faces of downtown high-rises long ago became home to the rock dove, more familiarly known as the pigeon, and the peregrine falcon has found a habitat niche amid city skyscrapers in recent years.

Power poles and fences, dams and reservoirs, and sprawling urban growth have all had a plus-and-minus effect on the bird population. But there's no avoiding the fact that pollution of our air, water, and land—and the ongoing loss of habitat as civilization encroaches—have threatened bird life worldwide and continue to do so.

One of the satisfactions of backyard bird-watching is that, by cultivating a habitat to attract birds, you can contribute in a small but valuable way to reclaiming the natural world for wildlife. To start, this may mean nothing more than allowing a few brambles to grow in a garden corner or planting a flower patch especially for hummingbirds. But when many such birdscaped areas are combined, the resulting patchwork can begin to offset some of the habitat losses caused by the relentless advance of civilization.

LIFE ON THE EDGE

In nature, the greatest mix of bird species occurs where two or more different habitats come together in borders of mixed vegetation referred to as "edges" or "ecotones." A field joins the willows and cattails on a pond's bank, for instance, or a forest opens into a meadow—tall trees giving way to shorter ones, these in turn merging with shrubbery that rambles into a grassy clearing.

As a gardener for birds, your goal is to imitate the arrangement of plants that occurs where a woodland makes the transition to grassland. This "edge," whether natural or purposefully created in a garden, encompasses habitats for many different birds.

With the right mix of trees, shrubs, vines, ground cover, and lawn, the needs of many species can be met. A flock of warblers may feed on tree-dwelling insects before flying south for winter. A month later, cedar waxwings and robins may descend to dine on a vine's newly ripened berries. As nuthatches glean insects from tree branches, finches find seeds on the ground below, fleeing to cover in thorny shrubs when a cat prowls near. Spring brings a hummingbird, scouting for a place to build its nearly invisible lichen and cobweb nest.

A woodsy garden lures birds with flowers and shrubs meandering toward the trees. Blooming plants include bee balm, coreopsis, and rudbeckia.

HOME, SWEET HABITAT

Birds have adapted to almost every imaginable habitat, from arctic tundra to tropical rain forest to towering cityscape. Even the birds that commonly visit backyards—only a fraction of the world bird population—are accustomed to widely varied habitats. Nonetheless, to attract birds to your garden habitat in the greatest possible number and diversity, you'll want to provide for the needs of the birds of your particular locality.

Start by understanding the four essential resources that any habitat must supply, be it coastal wetland or open prairie: food, water, shelter (protective cover), and a safe place to raise young.

A female purple finch savors a bud from a dogwood tree *(Cornus mas).*

FOOD. Plants in your garden can supply birds with a broad spectrum of foods: berries and other fruits, nuts, nectar, and the seeds of grasses, annual and perennial flowers, even shrubs and trees—and weeds. A garden buffet of insects and other invertebrates—from earthworms and caterpillars to flies, aphids, and tiny mites—provides important dietary protein for some species. Even birds that don't normally eat insects will forage for them during the breeding season when they have nestlings to feed. (For information on supplemental feeding of backyard birds, see page 20.)

WATER. Water for drinking is a daily necessity—as essential as food. Almost equally important is shallow water for bathing. A water source designed for birds and situated within quick reach of cover is a powerful attraction for a wide assortment of birds. (For guidelines on providing water, see page 32.)

SHELTER AND COVER. Birds rely on plants both for shelter from the elements and for protection from predators.

Shelter can mean relief from the midday sun or a place to roost for the night—or refuge from rain, wind, or freezing cold. Almost anything leafy will serve for shade or an overnight stay, but a heavier foliage canopy is needed to shield against harsher elements.

Where winter temperatures drop to zero or below, needle-leafed evergreen trees and shrubs are a must for the birds that stay in the area. Even in milder climates, dense, broad-leafed evergreen trees, shrubs, and vines will be appreciated for year-round shelter from rain and wind.

Depending on the predators they're evading, birds seek different kinds of protective cover. A convenient tree limb can give ample protection from a hawk. Thick shrubbery makes a good hideaway from a cat, as long as it's open enough for quick entry by a bird, yet dense enough to slow down or thwart the feline hunter. Thorns can turn a foliage hideaway into a real sanctuary, effectively deterring predators. And even better than a single shrub is a grouping that approximates a natural thicket. (See page 45 for other suggestions for foiling predators.)

Come on in! A female eastern bluebird takes the plunge.

SAFE PASSAGE

The garden shown in the plan below hosts more than two dozen kinds of birds by virtue of its thoughtful landscaping.

A protective trail was planted between the neighbor's willow tree (upper left) and the feeders outside the kitchen window (lower right). Ground-feeding birds travel low along the route in dense shrubbery; pine siskins, chickadees, and kinglets approach the feeders via the sides and tops of trees. Bushtits and various warblers simply work the plants themselves, ignoring the feeders.

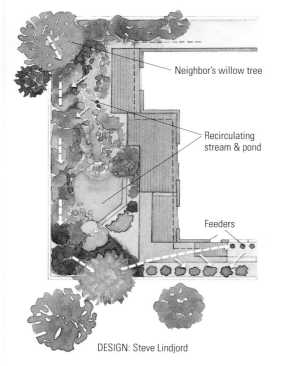

Neighbor's willow tree

Recirculating stream & pond

Feeders

DESIGN: Steve Lindjord

NESTING SITES. Birds use as many different styles of housing as do humans. Some nest on the ground, in grasses or under foliage. Some build nests in shrubbery at various heights. Others prefer "high-rise" accommodations—from tree limbs or cavities in tree trunks to nooks and ledges on buildings. Rock walls, hedgerows, fence posts, barns, rooftops, and chimneys are all places where birds find niches for nests.

Some birds breed comfortably in urban and suburban environments; others nest in remote areas, visiting a residential garden only for food or water—or during migration. Persuading birds to nest in your garden will give you a front-row seat to a far broader range of bird activity than if the birds come just to eat and drink. You can design a birdscape to offer nesting sites both in the plants you select and in man-made nest boxes (see page 38). Even dead trees or downed limbs are potentially attractive nest sites.

Dense evergreen branches make a sheltered hideaway for a chipping sparrow's nest.

BIRDER OR BIRD-WATCHER?

A relatively casual interest is what usually distinguishes "bird-watchers" from "birders," as the two terms are commonly used in birding parlance. A bird-watcher may join a local chapter of the Audubon Society to take field trips, attend programs, or participate in a bird count—or travel no farther than a backyard feeder and birdbath.

If you join the fraternity of birders, on the other hand, you'll take your place with a somewhat more zealous breed. Also known as field ornithologists, birders pursue detailed knowledge of birds that can be quite amazing—such as an ability to whistle precise birdsongs or identify wild plants that are favored by certain species.

Birders often focus on special interests: studying nest-building or migration patterns, for instance, or photographing birds. Some birders devote themselves to conservation efforts, and some travel the globe to add birds to their "life lists," records of every species they've ever identified.

COUNTING THE BIRDS

It's not a simple matter to collect data on a population that won't stay still. But scientists have enlisted the aid of bird-watching volunteers all across the continent to help with the task.

CHRISTMAS BIRD COUNT. In a tradition that began in 1900, volunteers methodically count birds for the National Audubon Society every year during the two weeks before and after Christmas. Counts are held in every U.S. state and Canadian province, in Central America, and parts of South America. Each count covers a 15-mile-diameter circle and takes place within a single 24-hour period.

Scientists use this data to assess the impact of environmental changes and to track population trends and range fluctuations. To learn how you can take part, contact the National Audubon Society (see page 126) or your local Audubon Society chapter.

A northern cardinal stands up to be counted during the annual Christmastime bird tally.

GREAT BACKYARD BIRD COUNT. In February, 1998, thousands of bird enthusiasts across the continent took part in the first Great Backyard Bird Count (GBBC), identifying more than a half-million birds at feeders, parks, and natural areas. This has become an annual event with several sponsors, including the Cornell University Laboratory of Ornithology (see page 126). The GBBC quickly compiles data and displays maps and tables on its website to create a "snapshot" of the birds that winter in North America.

PROJECT FEEDERWATCH. Backyard birders across the United States and Canada count individual birds and species every two weeks from November to March in a study sponsored by the Cornell University Laboratory of Ornithology. Begun in 1987, the project is funded by the participants, to help scientists analyze bird populations and health.

A rich habitat for birds has been created on this property. A pond, bordering flowers, and a backdrop of shrubs and trees are all within view of a bird-watcher's swinging perch. Lining the pond are marigold, phlox, rudbeckia, amaranth, hollyhock, and musk mallow.

Consider how your arrangement will look from the house or deck and from within the garden itself. Will you have a good view of the bird activity you hope to attract? To help you visualize your design, you can transfer it to the actual ground of the garden by outlining your planting areas with powdered gypsum or even flour. If the arrangement doesn't look right, just erase it with water and start over.

Once your plan shows everything more or less as you want it, you can pinpoint exactly which trees, shrubs, and other plants you want to add. Draw a circle to represent the width of each tree canopy and shrub. You'll be able to plant under most trees within a certain distance of the trunk unless surface roots interfere; check a reliable garden guide or consult nursery personnel for advice.

BIRDSCAPING YOUR GARDEN

Consider your bird garden an ongoing project. As your birdscape evolves, notice what works well and what is less successful. Let the birds rate your choices, and proceed accordingly—keeping in mind that it will take time for birds to discover and begin to use the habitat you've created.

PLAN, THEN PLANT

Whether you're starting from scratch or redesigning an existing garden to convert it into a birdscape, begin by assessing your site. Sketch your garden to scale on graph paper; 1 inch to 2 or 4 feet are common scales, but use whatever measure is convenient for you. Draw in the outline of your house and any outdoor structures such as patios, walks, and fencing.

Note features that will influence your plant selection, such as sunny and shady areas, slopes, or changes in soil quality. Mark the location of existing plants that you want to keep and neighbor's plants that will contribute to your birdscape.

Now you can begin to experiment. Tape tracing paper over your site map and try out different designs, sketching in "bubbles" to indicate trees, shrubs, vines, pools, and so on. Rough in the biggest trees first, to create the framework for your design, then add smaller trees and shrubs, vines, ground covers, and flower borders.

Towering spikes of hollyhocks planted right outside a window can lure nectar-seeking hummingbirds for close-up viewing.

A buffet of seeds and nectar is spread out for birds along this flagstone path in the form of blossoming verbena, bee balm *(Monarda),* phlox, salvia, and purple coneflower *(Echinacea,* both white and purple).

WHICH PLANTS?

Before you decide which trees and shrubs to plant, consider the birds you hope to attract. What are the resident species in your area? What migrating birds are temporary visitors? Watch and listen for birds in parks and gardens near your home, noting the trees, shrubs, vines, and ground covers where they prefer to congregate. Talk to birders or solicit suggestions from your county's Cooperative Extension Office, the local chapter of the Audubon Society, or an ecology center. Visit a good local nursery, arboretum, or botanical garden to see plants especially well-suited to your area.

Use the plant descriptions beginning on page 46 for guidance, and consult the "Garden Guest List" on pages 85–125 to learn the preferences of the birds you want to attract—for nesting sites as well as food.

Choose plants that will attract birds throughout the seasons. Of course, you'll want your plants to look attractive in your garden and thrive in your climate and sun conditions. Plants native to your region are the logical group to consider first. You know they're adapted to your climate and are familiar to your resident bird population.

You'll also want plants that can grow and mingle with as little restrictive pruning as possible. If you keep in mind the ultimate sizes of the plants when you lay out your garden, you'll be able to respect their natural growth habits as the garden develops.

Are there any existing plants you don't want to keep? To increase the diversity of plant material in your garden or to replace a plant that has little appeal for birds, you may want to remove some existing specimens.

FRUITING HEDGEROWS

Hedgerows between properties or along roadways in rural areas have offered food and shelter to birds for centuries. You can replicate this old-fashioned idea by planting a fruiting hedge as a screen in your garden. Or transform a shrub border by replacing fruitless plants with those that birds love. Combine serviceberry, blueberry, raspberry, bush cherry, and elderberry plants to produce a real fruit salad for birds. For a denser hedge, add holly, hawthorn, and rugosa roses.

After the rose blossoms fade, rose hips are tasty fare for birds.

MAKING IT OFFICIAL

One way to show that you're serious about supporting wild birds is to have your garden certified as an official Backyard Wildlife Habitat. This program, operated by the National Wildlife Federation, now includes many thousands of certified participants across the country. For information, contact the NWF (see page 126).

A spruce tree offers shelter and seeds for a tufted titmouse.

Jumbled greenery provides cover at various heights—and birdhouses hung from curly willow branches anchored in concrete give a choice of accommodations.

DESIGN BASICS

Let the following principles guide you in turning your garden into a birdscape:

∾ Plant some or all of the birdscape border with varied trees and shrubs, or begin your garden design where trees and shrubs are already established. Let large shade trees—either your own or your neighbor's—provide a canopy; shorter trees, an understory. Plan for shrubbery to emerge from the trees to form a bridge into open space.

∾ Diversity is the key to a birdscape with wide appeal. A design based on the repeated use of just a few plants will produce a habitat of limited value as far as birds are concerned. Instead, aim for a smorgasbord effect.

∾ Plan for succeeding and overlapping seasons of usefulness. Plants that offer variety in flowers, fruit, and foliage throughout the year will present changing views for you while giving birds a full range of foods and habitat conditions.

∾ In cold-winter regions, a stand of dense, needle-leafed evergreen trees will provide critical winter shelter. If possible, position these trees at the northern edge of the garden so they don't block winter sun. If your birdscape won't accommodate trees, consider a sheltering hedge of hemlock *(Tsuga)*.

∾ Include a garden oasis, however small, where water is available to birds (see page 32).

BIRDS, BUGS, AND PESTICIDES

A Carolina chickadee brings a caterpillar home for dinner.

Though gardeners may see insects as adversaries, for many birds they're simply something to eat. Birds classified as insectivores dine almost exclusively on insects, busily exploring every nook and cranny for beetles, worms, flies, mosquitoes, and more—even the eggs of insects. When nestlings need food, the interest in protein-rich insects rises sharply among other birds as well.

A female indigo bunting presents a protein snack to her hungry nestlings.

Some trees and shrubs routinely attract insects that lure birds. Resident insects of alder, birch, buckthorn, dogwood, hawthorn, maple, and oak trees make these trees particularly attractive to some birds. Insect-populated shrubs to consider planting include buckthorn, dogwood, honeysuckle, and manzanita.

Although you can't expect birds to eliminate all harmful insects from your garden, they can keep insects at a tolerable level for the health and appearance of your plants. Keep in mind that using pesticides—even natural ones—to rid your garden of harmful insects will also kill the insects that birds count on for food. The safest and most welcoming backyard habitat for birds is an organically gardened one. Eliminating pesticides is the most important thing you can do to make your yard bird-friendly. If you occasionally need to combat an exploded population of a damaging insect (mites or scale, for example), always choose the least toxic spray option, follow directions to the letter, and spray only infested plants.

JUST A TRIM, PLEASE

When you do any necessary pruning in your garden, make sure you're not disturbing nesting activity. With the right selection of plants, pruning chores should be minimal, but you might consider some seasonal shrub pruning to encourage denser branching, creating more branch crotches for nest niches.

To keep birds safe from chemical pollution, do not use insecticides, pesticides, fungicides, or herbicides while maintaining a feeding station. If you must spray, phase out feeding by at least one week before using toxic products, and don't resume feeding until after the contamination period specified on the product label. Unless it has rained since the spraying, water the garden well to wash vegetation before you start feeding again.

ON THE WILD SIDE

If your garden is "squeaky clean," it's not a paradise for birds. The impeccably manicured landscape—constantly raked, mowed, pruned, and sprayed for pests—usually offers little to attract birds and even less to hold their interest. A garden that approximates a wild, natural environment is far more likely to catch birds' attention. Here are a few ideas for achieving this:

- If you can spare a garden corner just for the birds, allow a "wild area" to develop. Let grasses grow high to produce seeds and create a congenial dining spot for ground-feeding species. Let a thorny, dense shrub (*Rosa multiflora,* for example, or a *Rubus* bramble such as blackberry) grow into a tangled thicket for nesting and refuge. Or let vines scramble through and over massed shrubbery.

- If a tree dies or drops a limb, let the wood decay naturally; birds will savor its insect population and may use the tree for nesting.

- Leave some patches of bare earth or sand in protected places. Dust baths are part of birds' grooming routines and probably help them to remove parasites and excess oil.

This brush pile offers safe haven from a curious dog. It remains green all year because of the flowering vines planted to clamber over the piled branches.

- Turn prunings into a brush pile. Birds will likely find refuge there from wandering cats and dogs, take shelter in harsh weather, and even nest among the branches.

  In an out-of-the-way place, pile pruned tree branches, grapevines, rose clippings, and so on into a dome 3 or 4 feet tall, using the larger pieces as a base. For year-round greenery in mild climates, you could plant rugged vines—like thorny Cherokee rose *(Rosa laevigata)* and purple-flowered honeysuckle (*Lonicera japonica* 'Purpurea')— to scramble over the pile. Or recycle Christmas trees by draping cut boughs on the pile. If you plan to dismantle your brush pile for the summer, do so before nesting activity begins in the spring.

WHAT ABOUT LAWNS?

Lawns provide play areas for people and add spaciousness to gardens, but in themselves they offer little to most birds. Some birds may swoop over in search of insects, and robins and flickers may probe for worms after a rain. But to most birds, an expanse of closely cropped grass represents vulnerability to predators. You can lure far more species if you rethink the nature of your lawn.

Look for ways to create islands of food-producing plants within your lawn and borders of plants around the edges. Think of your lawn as the center of a biological community, a habitat with food, water, and shelter that birds will recognize and frequent. Birds will use it as a flight path between plantings.

Here are a few hints to help you turn your lawn area into a birdscape:

- Restrict pesticide and herbicide applications—even organic ones. You'll be safeguarding the bugs, beetles, and larvae that feed birds.

- Instead of a traditional greensward, let your lawn area become an informal meadow with a few weeds, wildflowers, and clovers—a low-maintenance and environmentally friendly option. Or replace part of your lawn with a seed-bearing or fruiting ground cover, such as wild strawberry *(Fragaria chiloensis, F. virginiana).*

- Don't keep your lawn cropped too closely; taller grass provides habitat for more creatures that birds can eat.

- Interrupt your lawn by planting a tall tree or two. If there isn't room for a wide canopy, opt for a columnar variety; try to include at least one conifer.

- Choose several varieties of shrubs and a few multistemmed small trees to build foliage layers of various heights around your lawn. Birds can quickly seek refuge from predators in the protective branches.

Three Gardens for Birds

On the following four pages we offer three planting schemes specifically designed to attract birds. You can adapt these garden plans to your own space either by recreating them as shown or by using some of the suggested plants and substituting your own selections for others, depending on climate and personal preference. Or you can simply use these gardens as inspiration for your own ideas.

These garden plans demonstrate design principles discussed in the preceding pages: diversity of plant material, varied plant heights, and usefulness to birds over more than a single season. Of course, the gardens are also planned with an eye to providing a pleasing backdrop for bird-watching.

American goldfinch female perches on seed-rich purple coneflower.

Imitating a Woodland Edge

This expansive garden, illustrated here in its early autumn glory, offers just about everything birds need. For food, most of the trees and shrubs yield berries from late summer through winter; the birches, perennial flowers, and moor grass bear abundant seeds; the birches and viburnums are likely to host aphids—bane of gardeners but beloved of insect-eating birds. An elevated birdbath provides a safe spot for a drink and a splash; the cotoneaster shrubbery at its base is dense enough to discourage cats. Shrubs and trees create a multitude of places to take cover and to build nests; the thorny stems of the barberry and Washington thorn offer added protection.

The size of this planting scheme makes it suitable for larger properties where it would serve well as a transition from maintained yard to open field or woods—the type of "edge" planting likely to attract the greatest number of bird species. Many of these plants need at least a bit of winter chill (below freezing), but they won't withstand temperatures below −20° F/−29° C.

DESIGN: Philip Edinger

Numbers in parentheses indicate how many of each kind of plant are used in the garden plan.

Garden plan: 60' x 27'

Yellow-rumped warbler feasts on juniper berries.

PLANT LIST

A. **Betula nigra 'Heritage'.**
River birch (3+)

B. **Crataegus phaenopyrum.**
Washington thorn (3)

C. **Juniperus chinensis 'Hetz's Columnaris'.** Chinese juniper (1)

D. **Viburnum plicatum tomentosum 'Shasta'.** Doublefile viburnum (1)

E. **Euonymus alata.**
Winged euonymus (1)

F. **Amelanchier alnifolia.**
Saskatoon (1)

G. **Viburnum opulus 'Compactum'.**
European cranberry bush (1)

H. **Berberis thunbergii 'Atropurpurea'.**
Red-leaf Japanese barberry (2)

I. **Aronia arbutifolia.** Red chokeberry (2)

J. **Cotoneaster adpressus praecox** (3)

K. **Cotoneaster apiculatus.**
Cranberry cotoneaster (2)

L. **Cotoneaster dammeri.**
Bearberry cotoneaster (3)

M. **Echinacea purpurea.**
Purple coneflower (12)

N. **Coreopsis grandiflora 'Sunburst'** (12)

O. **Molinia caerulea.**
Purple moor grass (4)

A CORNER FOR BIRDS

A scaled-down plan for mild western climates, this informal corner garden offers the same inducements as the large garden on the previous two pages: berries, seeds, and shelter. There are no trees, but the shrubs will grow to a good size—about 10 feet for the elaeagnus, 8 feet for the pyracantha. One irresistible lure for birds is the pyracantha's yearly crop of berries ripening in late summer or fall. Birds will also feast on the fruits of lantana, heavenly bamboo, cotoneaster, and elaeagnus (in spring) and on the seeds of coreopsis, blanket flower, rudbeckia, and fountain grass. The shrubs all afford shelter—with the further protection of spines on the pyracantha. With a birdbath or other water source nearby, all the essentials will be provided.

This plan was designed for mild-winter regions of California and Arizona, but it can easily be adapted to a wider range of climate zones by substituting hardier plants for the lantana and the fountain grass.

DESIGN: Philip Edinger

PLANT LIST

A. Elaeagnus ebbingei (1)

B. Pyracantha coccinea 'Kasan'. Firethorn (1)

C. Lantana 'Radiation' (3+)

D. Nandina domestica.
Heavenly bamboo (2)

E. Cotoneaster salicifolius 'Emerald Carpet'.
Willowleaf cotoneaster (2+)

F. Rudbeckia fulgida 'Goldsturm'.
Black-eyed Susan (11)

G. Pennisetum setaceum. Fountain grass (6)

H. Gaillardia × grandiflora. Blanket flower (5)

I. Coreopsis grandiflora 'Sunburst' (4)

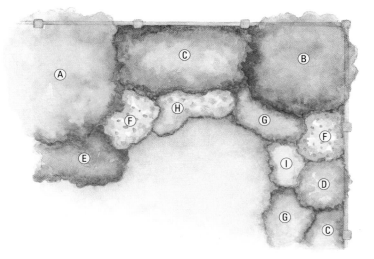

Garden plan: 25' x 18'

Calling All Hummingbirds

This colorful nook invites humans to simply sit and enjoy the vivid floral tapestry, but to hummingbirds it's a virtual beacon to a banquet. Blossom hues emphasize hummers' favorite reds and blues, and all the flowers contain generous stores of nectar—enabling the tiny winged dynamos to refuel. Best of all, this mixture of blooming plants will lure hummingbirds over a prolonged period, from mid- or late spring through the summer and possibly even into fall. The plants assembled in this garden plan will thrive over a large portion of good hummingbird territory, except for the southern Pacific Coast and low desert and the lower South.

DESIGN: Philip Edinger

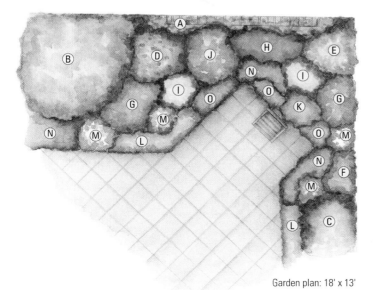

Garden plan: 18' x 13'

PLANT LIST

A. **Lonicera periclymenum 'Serotina'.** Woodbine (1)

B. **Weigela florida 'Bristol Ruby'** (1)

C. **Weigela florida 'Minuet'** (1)

D. **Monarda didyma 'Jacob Cline'.** Bee balm (6)

E. **Alcea rosea (Althaea rosea).** Hollyhock (7)

F. **Digitalis × mertonensis.** Foxglove (4)

G. **Agastache foeniculum.** Anise hyssop (9)

H. **Penstemon barbatus 'Prairie Fire'** (4)

I. **Asclepias tuberosa.** Butterfly weed (3)

J. **Salvia × superba 'Blue Hill'** (6)

K. **Lychnis chalcedonica.** Maltese cross (4)

L. **Heuchera sanguinea.** Coral bells (9+)

M. **Nicotiana alata, Nicki strain (mixed colors).** Flowering tobacco (12)

N. **Salvia splendens, dwarf red strain.** Scarlet sage (16)

O. **Petunia × hybrida, blue or purple** (8)

PROVIDING THE
ESSENTIALS

To entice the flash of wings to your backyard, you'll need to provide birds with the three things they need most: food, water, and shelter. These necessities of life will be supplied in part by garden planning (discussed in the previous chapter) and by your selection of plants (covered in the following chapter). But you can make your garden irresistible by supplementing the natural resources it provides.

Become knowledgeable about the kinds of birds that come into your yard or neighborhood now. Begin by catering to their tastes in food and housing. You can put up the best purple martin house in the world—but if you don't have purple martins where you live, you won't attract the tenants you're seeking. Birds tend to attract more birds, so once your yard becomes known as a dependable supplier of bed, bath, and board, you'll probably see expanding numbers—and species—arriving to take advantage of what you have to offer.

You can purchase a whole spectrum of attractive bird feeders, birdbaths, and birdhouses, or you may want to undertake some as do-it-yourself projects. In the following pages, you'll find basic guidelines to help you choose or create the right ones for the birds in your garden.

Cool water on a warm day brings an American robin to a
terra-cotta bath with a glazed bottom. The textured rim provides a good perching surface;
the saucer slips off of its pedestal for easy cleaning.

On a cold and snowy morning, tiers of pine siskins welcome a meal of hulled sunflower seeds.

PATIENCE REQUIRED

If your feeding station is new, expect several weeks to pass before the birds find it. They may return more promptly in subsequent years. The first customers to show up will probably belong to the most common species in your area. Others will eventually notice the commotion and join in.

Don't give up until you have tried offering black oil sunflower seeds, a favorite of many species, or scattering scraps of day-old bread or doughnuts on the ground.

FOOD AND FEEDERS

Supplemental feeding increases your garden's powers of attraction simply because nature can't usually match the concentrated supply of food that you can provide. Birds often remember where they had a good meal many months before, and they will return to the same spot for more.

Whether birds flock to your feeders seasonally or all year long, catering a banquet for them can be wonderfully satisfying, bringing life and color to the garden. In harsh winter climates, you're doing the birds a real service by keeping feeders supplied.

WHEN TO FEED

Most people who keep feeding stations do so in the fall, winter, and early spring. Birds need supplemental feeding the most in winter; feeders may provide the only winter food in severe climates.

Your winter feeding station will be most beneficial if you follow these guidelines:

- Set up feeders in September or October to attract birds as they begin to establish winter feeding territories.

- Place feeders on the south side of your house, if possible, to catch winter sun. Moist food will dry faster in sunlight.

- If you don't plan to feed all winter long, don't stop suddenly. Cut down gradually by about ¼ per week over a period of several weeks, until the birds have become less dependent on your feeding station.

- Unless you plan to keep feeding through the warm season, gradually reduce feed and then remove feeders between March and May, before birds become territorial in spring.

- Set out food if an unseasonable freeze occurs after you've stopped feeding. Continue feeding until natural food sources are available again.

Will the birds become dependent on your seed? Some believe that, if you encourage migrant birds to stay through a harsh winter by feeding them through autumn, they may perish if you stop. With the excellent survival skills of wild creatures, most lingering migrants would probably be able to forage from nearby feeders or other food sources if your supply ran out. A severe snowstorm might be too much for them, however. If you don't plan to feed through the winter, it's best to decrease the flow gradually so that birds become accustomed to seeking food elsewhere.

During spring and summer, feeding stations often become somewhat less popular with birds, probably because then they're territorial and chase rivals away. And the seeds, berries, nuts, or insects available naturally during the growing season are more appetizing to birds than most supplemental foods. Many species that rely on seeds during the fall and winter shift to insects during the breeding season. However, if you choose to keep feeding, the birds you attract may make you a privileged observer of spring and summer nesting activities.

SECRETS OF SUCCESS

What could be simpler than feeding birds? Just toss some bread crumbs on the ground, and at least a few birds are bound to notice. Actually, there's a bit more to it than that. The following tips will help you to maintain a successful feeding station:

- To avoid spreading avian diseases, maintain clean equipment and fresh food supplies. Clean feeders with mild soap and hot water before setting them out the first time; rinse and dry thoroughly. Clean again if feeders get wet and have seed stuck to the corners; using a weak bleach solution will eliminate disease-causing bacteria. Clean suet feeders often if the weather is warm enough to melt suet, and clean any feeder if you suspect that food has spoiled in it.

- Plan for how much food you wish (and can afford) to dispense per day. Up to a point, birds will eat as much as you provide once a feeding station is established.

- Feed early in the morning, when birds are most active and are hungry for high-energy food.

- Use the right feeders to avoid waste—thistle seed feeders for thistle (Niger) seed, for example, and suet feeders for suet. Choose feeders for small birds that discourage use by larger birds.

Continued on page 22 >

ABOVE: Goldfinches flock to a tube feeder enclosed in a metal grid designed to keep out larger birds and squirrels.

BELOW: Different types of feeders at varied heights accommodate many bird species.

FEEDER FAVORITES

Black-capped chickadee

What do birds like best to eat? Some, like finches and sparrows, depend mainly on seeds all year. Others patronize seed feeders during much of the year but seek out insects when their nestlings need protein. Insects are the year-round preferred diet of woodpeckers and warblers, among others, but these birds can be attracted to gardens by suet—or even fruit.

These are the preferred foods of some backyard birds:

CARDINALS: Black oil sunflower and safflower seeds are the first choices, but other seeds will attract if the favorites aren't available. Year-round residents in most of their range, these birds may approach both ground feeders and raised trays and dispensers.

CHICKADEES AND TITMICE: These birds love sunflower seeds! Suet and peanut butter mixed with cornmeal (see pages 24–25) also have big appeal—especially in winter. Titmice also particularly relish safflower seeds. Set out very small feeders to thwart competition from large birds.

DOVES: These ground feeders appreciate sunflower and safflower seeds, cracked corn, chicken scratch, and peanut hearts, provided on the ground or on a table feeder.

FINCHES: House and purple finches devour mixed seeds, with a preference for millet, sunflower, and safflower. They'll feed on the ground, at a raised tray or table, or from a hanging dispenser.

GOLDFINCHES AND SISKINS: Sunflower or thistle (Niger) seeds may draw these birds.

HUMMINGBIRDS: Those that come to feeders take only sugar water (see page 27).

ORIOLES: Though shy at the feeder, orioles may be lured in winter by fruit. They may also visit sugar-water feeders that offer perching space and large enough ports to accommodate their beaks.

QUAIL: Feeder trays and ground-feeding areas are likely to bring these birds; try spreading chicken scratch near cover.

SPARROWS AND JUNCOS: Mixed seeds attract native sparrows and juncos. Visiting gardens mainly in winter, these birds may be rather shy ground feeders at first, but they may alight on your deck or a raised feeding tray as they grow more comfortable.

WOODPECKERS: Suet is the primary backyard attraction, mainly in fall and winter; offer it in a mesh bag or suet cage attached to a tree or post. Woodpeckers may be interested in sugar-water feeders, fruit, and nutmeats, too.

CRACKING THE CASE

Seed-eating birds such as grosbeaks have heavy bills that can easily crack seed hulls open. But some insectivores also eat seeds, especially when the insect supply is low. Lacking a bill strong enough to crack a seed, an insectivore such as a chickadee holds the seed down with one foot and hammers it open with its bill.

Dried corn on the cob, raised on a post, makes a hit with a red-bellied woodpecker.

NO SPROUTING

Stop stray birdseed from sprouting in your garden by cooking it first to prevent germination. Simply spread birdseed in a thin layer (about ¼-inch thick) on a cookie sheet with raised sides. Bake for 8 minutes in a 300° oven; cool seed completely before pouring it into feeders.

Baking sterilizes the seed but doesn't affect the nutritional value. This procedure isn't necessary for thistle (Niger) seed, which is commercially sterilized before you buy it.

Nonsprouting seed mixes are also available from bird-feeding suppliers.

༄ Avoid overfeeding; if you put out more food than birds can eat in a day, the leftovers may attract squirrels, mice, rats, and unwanted bird species. Put out only as much suet as birds can finish within a few days, or else it may turn rancid.

༄ Don't let feed collect on the ground; rotting seed can cause disease and can sprout as weeds. Position feeders over a deck or masonry for easiest cleanup, or hang them over a ground cover that discourages sprouting.

༄ Offer different types of seeds in separate feeders so that birds won't waste the kinds of seeds they don't like—and you can discourage birds you don't want around, if need be, by removing their preferred seeds.

༄ To keep conflict to a minimum, place feeders for different kinds of birds in separate parts of your yard. If you provide for larger and more aggressive birds elsewhere, you can lure birds such as chickadees to a small feeder that you can see from indoors.

༄ Don't use insecticides, pesticides, fungicides, or herbicides while maintaining a feeding station (see pages 12–13).

SORTING OUT BIRDSEED

For vegetarian birds, seeds are nutritious meals, conveniently packaged. The oil in the seeds helps birds maintain body fat to sustain themselves in winter weather and furnishes calories for their constant activity. Seed protein is important for birds' strenuously worked muscles.

Sunflower seeds delight seed-eating birds almost anywhere, but other seeds vary in appeal from one locality to another. To find out what the birds in your neighborhood like best, experiment with small amounts of different seeds to see what disappears first.

Mixed birdseed is sold at many supermarkets and pet stores, but it's usually more economical to buy separate kinds in bulk from a bird supply or feed store, Audubon center, garden supplier, or mail-order supplier. The following seeds are all favorites; to find out what various species usually favor, see the chart on the facing page.

BLACK OIL SUNFLOWER SEED. This oil-rich seed is wildly popular with a wide range of birds. The tiny size and thin hulls of these seeds make them easy for small birds to handle.

STRIPED SUNFLOWER SEED. This is a popular, nutritionally rich food for birds with heavy bills. Offer it unmixed, or else sunflower seed–eating birds will just waste what you put out with it.

HULLED SUNFLOWER SEED. Attractive to smaller seedeaters, hulled sunflower seed leaves no mess under feeders—but it's expensive, and it may rot in wet weather.

WHITE PROSO MILLET. Both red and white millet are available, but birds generally prefer the white type. Its hard seed coat makes millet less prone to swelling and rotting than other seeds, thus making it useful for ground feeding as well as hopper feeders.

SAFFLOWER SEED. Known as a food for cardinals, safflower seed is also a favorite of titmice, finches, and mourning doves. It offers a special advantage: Squirrels usually leave it alone.

THISTLE (NIGER) SEED. High in protein and fat, this import from Africa and Asia in no way resembles the familiar thistle weed. The tiny black seeds, a favorite of small finches, are often dispensed from a special mesh sock or tube feeder to prevent spillage. Thistle seed is expensive, but it offers an added value in that it does *not* attract squirrels or blackbirds.

FRESH AND DRIED CORN. Cracked corn appeals to ground-feeding birds, but it does have disadvantages: It rots quickly if it gets wet, and it attracts squirrels, pigeons, blackbirds, and house sparrows. On or off the cob, whole corn kernels—fresh or dried—provide rich nourishment for larger birds.

BIRDSEED MIX. Seed mixes vary widely in composition, and supermarket mixes tend to include less appealing, inexpensive grains such as milo (grain sorghum), rice, oats, or wheat. (Starlings, often a nuisance in gardens, do love milo and hulled oats.) Avoid mixes with a reddish hue, evidence of too much milo—it will be wasted. Choose a mix with a pale yellow cast, indicative of corn and millet; the more sunflower seed, the better.

SEED PREFERENCES

SPECIES	THISTLE (NIGER) ①	CRACKED CORN ②	MIXED SEED ③	WHITE PROSO MILLET ④	BLACK OIL SUNFLOWER ⑤	HULLED SUNFLOWER ⑥	STRIPED SUNFLOWER ⑦	SAFFLOWER ⑧	SHELLED PEANUTS & HEARTS ⑨	PEANUTS IN SHELLS ⑩
Northern bobwhite		✦	✦	✦	✦	✦			✦	
Mourning dove	✦	✦	✦	✦	✦	✦		✦	✦	
Woodpeckers		✦			✦	✦	✦		✦	✦
Jays		✦	✦		✦	✦	✦	✦	✦	✦
Chickadees					✦	✦	✦	✦	✦	
Tufted titmouse					✦	✦	✦	✦	✦	
Towhees		✦	✦	✦	✦	✦				
Chipping sparrow	✦	✦	✦	✦	✦				✦	
Song sparrow	✦	✦	✦	✦	✦				✦	
White-crowned sparrow	✦	✦	✦	✦	✦	✦				
Dark-eyed junco	✦	✦	✦	✦	✦				✦	
Purple finch	✦		✦	✦	✦	✦	✦	✦		
House finch	✦		✦	✦	✦	✦	✦	✦		
Northern cardinal		✦	✦	✦	✦	✦		✦		
Pine siskin	✦		✦	✦	✦	✦			✦	
American goldfinch	✦			✦	✦	✦				
Evening grosbeak		✦	✦	✦	✦	✦	✦	✦		
House sparrow	✦	✦	✦	✦	✦	✦				

DIETARY SUPPLEMENTS

In a severe winter, snow and ice may prevent birds from tapping all the natural resources they need. You can supplement their food supply by offering gravel, ash, crushed eggshell, and salt.

Certain birds, such as mourning doves and finches, need grit—tiny bits of stone, coarse sand, or crushed oyster shell—to crush seeds in their crops. You can purchase grit at feed and pet stores.

Ash (from the fireplace) or crushed eggshell will function as grit and also replenish minerals that birds may lack during a harsh winter. Eggshells can also provide calcium during nesting season. (Rinse eggshells in warm water and dry in a warm oven.)

Coarse salt meets the sodium needs of some birds.

Provide grit, ash, and salt on covered feeding trays or on the ground. Mix crushed eggshell with seed or suet.

SIMPLE SUET FEEDERS

To keep large birds from carrying away more than their share of suet, you'll need to enclose it somehow. Many commercial suet feeders are available; you can also wrap suet with ½-inch wire mesh, put chunks in a string or mesh bag (the kind used for oranges or onions), or use a berry basket or wire soap dish as a suet cage to attach to a tree.

Dip a pinecone in melted suet, or drill 1-inch-diameter holes into (but not through) a small log and fill it with melted suet. Refrigerate to harden the suet, then hang from a tree limb. To attract birds that can't cling to tree trunks, you can insert small wooden dowel perches below some of the holes in your log feeder.

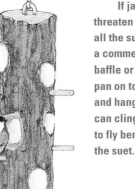

If jays and squirrels threaten to make off with all the suet, try attaching a commercial squirrel baffle or even a metal pie pan on top of your feeder and hanging it. Birds that can cling will still be able to fly beneath to reach the suet.

B EYOND B IRDSEED

Seeds aren't the only foods that will bring birds to your garden. Suet and peanuts are important attractions for many insectivores. Preparing occasional treats can be fun, too—and you may see your feathered clientele increase as more species show up to sample the specialties of your house. The following snacks are simple and quick to prepare. Watch your feeders to learn how well each offering is received.

SUET AND SUET CAKES

Suet is a favorite of such insect-eating birds as woodpeckers and mockingbirds, and it can be an important wintertime source of fat for birds in cold climates.

Suet is hard beef fat (best from beef kidneys); you can buy it at a meat market or bird-feeding store, or you can cut the fat off steaks or roasts before you cook them. To offer suet to birds, cut it into chunks about 2 inches square and place it in a mesh bag or other container. Don't offer regular suet in warm weather; it's likely to go rancid or melt, sticking to birds' feathers. No-melt suet, with a lower fat content, is available from bird-supply specialists.

Rendering suet expands the possibilities. Cut suet into small chunks to melt in a microwave oven or in a heavy pan over low heat on the stovetop. Pour the rendered suet into a small mold (such as an empty tuna can or a small muffin cup liner) and refrigerate to harden; unmold before offering it to birds. Or pour rendered suet over a pinecone to fill the crevices, refrigerate to harden, and hang.

Suet is harder and keeps longer after it is rendered. You can also offer rendered bacon fat in place of rendered suet.

SUET CAKES. Mix slightly cooled **rendered suet** with other favorite bird foods: a tablespoon or two of **peanut butter, cornmeal, oatmeal, chopped table scraps, dried fruit, or birdseed.** For grit and calcium, mix in **1 or 2 eggshells,** well crushed. Pour into paper-lined muffin cups or other molds and refrigerate until hardened, then unmold and set out in a mesh bag or on a tray.

PEANUTS AND PEANUT BUTTER

Peanuts and peanut butter mix are packed with protein and fat and can provide the extra nutrients that birds need in cold weather. In summer, these foods can strengthen insectivores for the demanding cycle of breeding and feeding young.

Offer only unsalted peanuts. Insectivores and seedeaters large enough to handle them—like jays and woodpeckers—enjoy peanuts in the shell; string a few on a wire to hang from a tree limb. Most birds need shelled

A Steller's jay prepares to crack open a peanut.

kernels or peanut hearts (removed during the process of making peanut butter), however. Starlings prefer peanut hearts to all else, so beware if these birds are aggressive in your garden.

Birds can choke on peanut butter by itself, so always mix it with another food to make it less sticky: 1 part peanut butter and 4 to 6 parts cornmeal or other cereal. And don't offer peanut butter when the weather is hot enough to melt it.

PEANUT BUTTER MIX. Mix **½ cup unsalted peanut butter** (either smooth or crunchy) with **2½ cups cornmeal or uncooked oatmeal,** blending well. If you wish, add about **¼ cup finely chopped leftover meat (in winter), dried fruit, or nutmeats.** With a rubber spatula, spread the mixture thickly on a pinecone or log feeder, such as the one shown opposite.

CORN PUDDING

Actually a rich version of suet cake, corn pudding disappears quickly in cold weather. In a deep bowl, mix together **4 cups water** and **2 cups sugar.** In a heavy pan over low heat, slowly melt **2 cups suet or lard;** allow it to cool slightly, then stir it into the sugar-water mixture, alternating with **4 cups yellow cornmeal,** until a soft dough forms. Gradually stir in **4 cups all-purpose flour** to make a stiff dough. Stuff the dough deep into the crevices of large pinecones to hang as feeders, or spread it onto a log feeder.

BIRD CAKES

These make nice treats for special occasions. Mix **1 cup all-purpose flour** with **1 cup cornmeal, oatmeal, or bread crumbs,** or a combination of all three. Moisten with **½ cup milk.** Enrich with about **1 cup raisins or peanuts,** or

TOP: A mesh bag provides suet—and a toe-hold—for a downy woodpecker.

CENTER: A tufted titmouse enjoys a nut feeder.

BOTTOM: A Baltimore oriole steps up to the juice bar.

both combined. Also blend in **½ cup rendered suet (or other fat) or peanut butter.**

Bake in paper-lined muffin cups at 350° for 45 to 60 minutes, or until the cakes are quite firm and brown. Cool, cut into sections, and present on a tray or in a mesh sack hung from a branch.

FRUIT TREATS

Fresh fruit will entice orioles, tanagers, thrushes, and other shy garden visitors. Just hammer a nail through a board that can be hung on a tree. Impale a section of banana or half of an apple or orange (cut side out) on the nail.

Grapes, cherries, or any dried fruits can be set out on feeding trays; a halved and hollowed-out grapefruit or orange can serve as a container. To make raisins tastier, soften them in water. Birds will appreciate an opened pomegranate, too—but offer it over a thicketed area to avoid a mess.

COCONUT DELIGHT

Start by piercing the dark "eyes" in the top of a **fresh coconut,** using an ice pick or screwdriver, then drain off the liquid inside. Place the coconut on a rimmed baking sheet and bake in a 350° oven for 15 minutes, or until the shell just starts to crack. Cool briefly, then break the coconut open by placing it on a hard surface and striking it along the crack with a hammer.

Fill the largest piece of coconut with **fruit, nutmeats, or crumbs of day-old bread, cake, or doughnuts.** Hang it by a string from a tree limb, nail it to the top of a fence post, or set it out on a feeding tray.

Use only fresh coconut. Packaged coconut flakes have been known to harm birds by swelling inside them.

RIGHT: Raisins on a mesh-bottomed tray feeder attract a northern mockingbird.

BELOW: A western scrub-jay picks seeds from a rustic covered platform that doubles as garden folk art.

LEFTOVERS FOR DINNER

Treats such as chunks of doughnut or stale poppyseed bagel, leftover corn-bread, or even dry dog food may attract birds quickly. But don't offer these items as a steady feeder diet, don't put out spoilable foods in hot weather, and don't leave your leftovers out long enough to attract rodents.

FEEDER BASICS

Locate feeders at varying levels to attract different birds, close enough to cover to allow escape from predators but not right next to shrubs where cats could lie in wait. Use feeders designed to protect seed from rain, snow, and garden sprinklers. Situate them where the wind won't blow seed away and birds will be protected from winter's chill. Keep suet out of direct sun, especially in warm weather, or else it may turn rancid.

You can choose traditional feeders of wood or more modern designs of sleek acrylic or lightweight metal—and all sorts of design styles, from whimsical to high tech. Just keep in mind the kind of food you'll be offering and the species of birds you want to attract (or discourage). Some feeders are designed for certain birds; by offering more than one type of feeder, you're bound to attract a wider clientele.

When selecting a feeder, evaluate how easy it will be to fill and clean it. Keeping feeders clean is imperative for the health of the birds you'll be feeding, so you'll want feeders that open easily for cleaning.

PLATFORMS. The most basic kind of feeder is a platform or tray feeder—a flat surface on which food is scattered. This is a good way to begin, because this type of feeder is quickly noticed by birds and appeals to many species—thus giving you a good snapshot of the birds in your neighborhood. You can refine your feeder approach once you know what species you are catering to.

A platform feeder might be as basic as a piece of plywood elevated on sawhorses or as elegant as

Continued on page 28 >

FEEDING HUMMINGBIRDS

There's something captivating about hummingbirds. As these tiny performers hang in midair, seemingly motionless, their wings beat faster than your eyes can register. You can bring the show right up to your window by offering humming-birds a sugar-water mixture that approximates the nectar they seek in flowers.

Hang sugar-water feeders by the time migrating humming-birds are due to arrive on their northward flight to breeding grounds—as early as mid-February in some places. How long you should leave feeders up depends on where you live. Even if hummers normally migrate south from your area in late summer or fall, there's no evidence that an artificial food supply will keep them from making their journey. In fact, a plentiful nectar supply allows them to stock up before a long migration. And not all hummers migrate; in some southern regions, they may hover at feeders all year long—depending on sugar water for sustenance when few nectar-bearing flowers are available.

Hang your nectar feeder in a shady spot that's safe from cats. To attract more hummingbirds, offer feeders in more than one location; thus territorial-minded hummers can stake out their own feeders. Try to locate feeders near plants that offer the nourishment of actual flower nectar (see page 70).

FEEDER MAINTENANCE. When selecting a feeder, consider the ease of cleaning it. Hummers can develop a deadly fungal infection if feeders are dirty, so you want to be sure yours makes this frequent necessity as simple as possible.

Never use honey in place of sugar in hummingbird nectar—it can cause a fungal infection. Don't add food coloring; a touch of red on the feeder itself is sufficient to catch hummers' attention. Change nectar at least weekly in cool weather—twice per week in warm weather.

Thoroughly clean feeders at least weekly; you've waited too long if the solution is cloudy or black mold has

formed. Use a mixture of 2 cups water, 1 teaspoon mild dishwashing liquid, and 2 tablespoons household bleach to scrub all feeder parts. If there's black algae inside that you can't reach, add a few tablespoons of sand to the cleaning solution and shake the feeder vigorously. Rinse thoroughly and dry.

If ants find your feeder, hang it from thin nylon fishing line or apply petroleum jelly to the hanging attachment. If the feeder draws bees, coat the openings with cooking oil; keep outside surfaces clean.

HUMMINGBIRD NECTAR

Combine **1 part granulated sugar** and **4 parts water** in a saucepan (⅓ cup sugar and 1⅓ cups water makes enough to fill two standard satellite feeders). Boil for 2 minutes, then allow to cool completely before using. Extra nectar can be stored in the refrigerator for several weeks.

Never make your nectar any sweeter than this ratio—too much sugar can result in a liver dysfunction.

Orioles also like sugar water, but they prefer **1 part sugar** to **6 parts water** (⅓ cup sugar to 2 cups water). To appeal to both hummers and orioles, try using 1 part sugar to 5 parts water.

A HUMMER FEEDER TO MAKE

You can construct a simple nectar feeder by fitting a bottle with a tight rubber stopper and a bent glass tube. A little searching at either a pet store or a scientific supply outlet should turn up both stopper and tube. Hummingbirds love red, so add some bright tape or an artificial red flower. You can fashion a holder out of wire to nail to a post or wall or attach to a hanger.

Twisted wire holder
Tapered rubber stopper
Bent glass tube
Red plastic flower

Goldfinches are enthusiastic diners either clinging to an acrylic globe (above) or perched at a column of seed in a square tube (right).

a copper-roofed gazebo mounted on a pole. To be most functional, the feeder should have raised edges to keep seed from being blown away and drainage holes or a mesh surface to let moisture run out. Even a folding TV tray makes a good platform feeder— if you punch holes for drainage, you've created a feeder that can be moved wherever you want it.

Platform feeders do have disadvantages. They need frequent cleaning, because seed hulls and bird droppings are deposited on the surface. Large birds tend to dominate these feeders. And birds are more vulnerable to predators on an open platform.

HOPPERS, TUBES, AND GLOBES. A longtime favorite, the hopper feeder has a storage bin so that seed automatically flows as it is needed. This kind of feeder attracts a varied following of bird species. Some hoppers have separate bins for differents kinds of seed, or suet or fruit holders in addition to seed bins.

The tube feeder, usually plastic, is a popular way to dispense black oil sunflower seed or thistle (Niger) seed, depending on the size of the holes. Tube feeders attract small birds such as finches, chickadees, and nuthatches. Don't fill them with mixed birdseed—the unwanted kinds of seeds will just be discarded. Tube feeders with metal perches and openings are the most durable.

A globe feeder attracts small clinging species, like chickadees and titmice—giving them their own private diner, since larger birds can't get a toehold on the feeder.

RECYCLE THOSE SEEDS!

"Exotic" birdseed can be salvaged from what you usually discard in the kitchen— such as fresh or dried seeds from pumpkins and other squashes, bell peppers, cucumbers, citrus fruit, papayas, pomegranates, and other fruits and vegetables. Save sesame, caraway, and poppy seeds along with crumbs from leftover baked goods. Add recycled seeds to any of the recipes on pages 24–25, or sprinkle tiny seeds, such as caraway or poppy seeds, on bird cakes before serving them.

OTHER FEEDERS. Acrylic seed feeders that attach to windows with suction cups are fun to watch from indoors, though they usually have limited capacity. Most are best suited to small birds. Window feeders for suet and hummingbird nectar are also available. Some window feeders have one-way backs so that birds can't see through and won't be frightened away by indoor bird-watchers—or you can buy a separate sheet of one-way screening material.

A window feeder provides a close-up of a chickadee.

LEFT: Rose-breasted grosbeaks share a feeder equipped with an acrylic dome to keep seed dry and a tray to catch spilled seed.

RIGHT: A white-breasted nuthatch navigates a feeder made to hold suet or peanut butter mixed with cornmeal or oatmeal.

A weighted-perch feeder is one of several models designed specifically to keep squirrels out. It closes under the weight of a squirrel but stays open when lightweight birds land. Other feeders are encased in metal cages that prevent squirrels or large birds from getting to the seed; small birds can hop through the metal grid.

Fine mesh bags are one way to offer thistle seed. Other specialized feeders are designed just for suet, nuts, corn, fruit, or hummingbird nectar; an oriole nectar feeder is similar to a hummer feeder, but it offers larger ports and a place to perch.

This satellite-style feeder holds sugar water for hummingbirds.

HARDWARE. For hanging and mounting feeders, you'll find poles, pivoting arms, and hangers at bird product outlets and through mail-order suppliers. Various kinds of baffles and slippery pole sleeves are available to keep raccoons, squirrels, and other rodents from emptying the feeder (also see page 45).

BULLIES, KEEP OUT

One way to discourage pigeons and cats from harassing small birds at a tray feeder is to create a canopy of heavy wire mesh. Use vinyl-coated garden wire with rectangular openings about 2 by 2½ inches—large enough for small birds to hop in and out. Arch a strip of the mesh over the feeding table, stapling it tightly along the two long sides so that large birds can't get in and become entangled. For a platform about 1½ feet wide, arch the wire mesh so that it's about 8 inches high over the middle of the feeder. Leave the ends open, enabling feeding birds to make a quick escape from predators. For maximum safety from cats, raise the tray on a pole.

REFLECTION PROTECTION

Don't position feeders where they might cause birds to fly into windows. Sky reflected in glass can be mistaken by birds for the real thing, resulting in injury. Fine netting, curtains, drapes, or blinds can help break up the reflection and prevent calamities. Some people use decals to steer birds in another direction; be sure to use enough of them to effectively break up the reflective surface. If you do locate a feeder near a window, place it close enough—within a foot or so—that birds won't build up enough speed to hurt themselves if they fly from the feeder toward the window.

CLASSIC HOPPER FEEDER

This tried-and-true feeder design keeps seeds dry until they are needed. This is a fairly large feeder, but you can scale down all the dimensions if you wish.

1 Cut 1 by 8 lumber to size for floor, side walls, and roof pieces, as indicated in the diagram. Cut 1 by 2 rails for sides and ends.

2 Drill $3/8$-inch holes through the end rails for perches; then nail both sets of rails to the floor. Insert dowel perches, adding a bit of waterproof glue to the holes; sand off excess dowel at ends.

3 Cut clear $1/8$-inch acrylic into two $7\frac{1}{2}$- by 13-inch sheets (for best results, use a paneling blade on a portable circular saw or table saw). Nail cleats in place to hold the acrylic at an angle against inside walls; we show $7/16$- by $7/8$-inch molding, but any similar wood pieces will work. Nail walls to base, predrill screw holes in acrylic pieces, and fasten acrylic to the cleats with screws and finishing washers.

4 Nail the roof pieces to the side walls, hinging one side as shown. If you wish, attach weather stripping inside the hinged section for added rain protection.

5 Mount the feeder on a galvanized steel pipe or a wooden post.

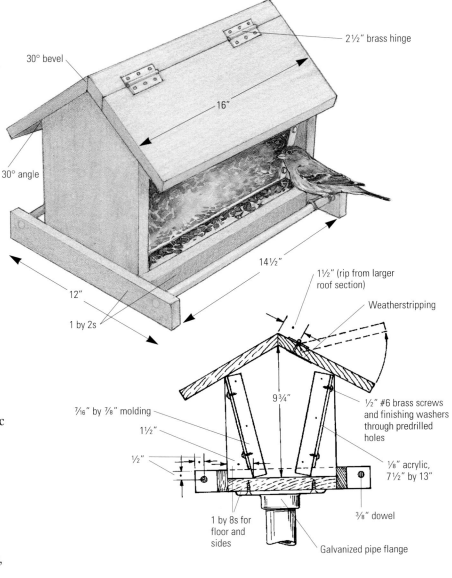

TOOLS AND MATERIALS

Most of the projects in this chapter are easy to put together using standard homeowner's tools—saw, measuring tape, drill, and hammer—although a portable circular saw and a jigsaw will make the work go more smoothly. A radial-arm saw and a table saw are great for crosscutting, ripping, and shaping the occasional bevel, but they aren't necessary. In many cases, you can substitute simple butt joints for trickier connections.

Decay-resistant redwood, cedar, and cypress are the most durable woods for bird feeders and houses, but you can use whatever scraps you have on hand. Don't bother to varnish, or even to sand smooth, unless the woodworker in you insists: Birds like their accommodations on the rough side. Experts also advise against paint—it doesn't appeal to birds, and some finishes are toxic.

Use rustproof nails, screws, mounting pipes, and hanging hardware.

A HOLIDAY TREE FOR BIRDS

If you live where the winters are freezing cold, birds will especially appreciate edible gifts during the Christmas season. Even in milder climates, a tree decorated for birds can be a special part of the seasonal celebration.

Whether you use a tree growing in your garden or recycle your family's Christmas tree as a post-holiday feeding station, keep in mind that winter feeding should provide a steady source of nutrients. When the decorations have been eaten, continue to offer food or, if you don't plan to feed through the winter, phase out feeding gradually (see page 20).

Ideally, decorate a tree that you can watch from the breakfast table. Make sure there's cover close by—shrubs or dense trees—in case birds need to flee.

The recipes on pages 24–25 can be adapted as tree ornaments, or you can try out these ideas:

- Garlands of popcorn (unbuttered and unsalted), cranberries, hawthorn or other berries, grapes, apple nuggets, or large nutmeats, strung on heavy-duty thread and tied to branches to keep them from slipping off

- Dried fruit pieces, hung individually or added to garlands

- Oranges and grapefruit, cut in quarters or slices and tied to branches

- Corn on the cob (dried or fresh), tied to strong branches

- Whole peanuts (unsalted), threaded garland-style or strung on wire loops

- Small pinecones dipped in rendered suet or stuffed with peanut butter mix (see pages 24–25) and coated with birdseed

- Stalks of ornamental wheat

It can take awhile for birds to discover your tree. To issue an invitation, put out some preferred birdseed—such as black sunflower seed—close to the decorated tree. Even a handful of seeds broadcast on the ground or placed on a platform feeder nearby can attract winter finches.

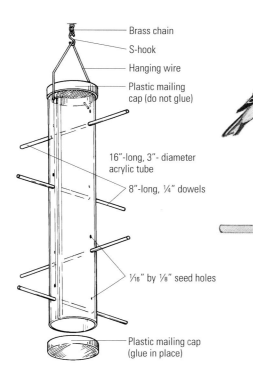

Brass chain
S-hook
Hanging wire
Plastic mailing cap (do not glue)

16"-long, 3"- diameter acrylic tube

8"-long, ¼" dowels

¹⁄₁₆" by ⅛" seed holes

Plastic mailing cap (glue in place)

THISTLE FEEDER

Acrylic tubing makes it easy to put together a homemade thistle feeder. Cut ⅛-inch-thick acrylic 16 inches long, and add two plastic caps—the bottom one glued in place, the top one loose for refilling.

To find acrylic tubing, look in the Yellow Pages under "Plastics: Rods, Tubes, Sheets, etc." Cut, drill, and sand the tube as needed. To make each tiny, elongated seed dispenser, drill a ¹⁄₁₆-inch hole, then let the drill "travel" a little up or down. Drill ¼-inch holes for dowel perches and smaller holes near the top to insert a hanging wire.

Hammer the dowels into place, then secure the bottom cap with epoxy. Hanging wire, brass chain, and an S-hook complete the hardware.

RIGHT: A shallow pool with a dripper adds to the bird appeal of this woodland shade garden.

BELOW: A Carolina chickadee stops off for a drink from a hanging birdbath.

THE LURE OF WATER

Water holds a powerful attraction for birds. By offering a place where they can drink and bathe, you'll greatly increase the number of resident and visiting birds in your garden. Birds will happily frolic in a puddle, but a birdbath in the right spot—kept full and clean—is the ultimate back-yard watering hole for all kinds of feathered friends.

The vessel itself isn't critical, as long as it is very shallow, slopes gently, and has a roughened surface to give birds a good foothold. Even an upside-down garbage can lid or a simple terra-cotta plant saucer can make a fine birdbath.

For your own enjoyment, position your birdbath where you can see it from your house or patio. For the birds' sake, choose a location sheltered from strong winds where the bath will get morning sun but midday shade (so the water doesn't get too warm).

BIRDBATH BASICS

Birdbaths can be made out of practically anything—concrete, glazed ceramic, metal, plastic, terra-cotta, stone, fiberglass, even wood. Plastic and metal withstand lots of weather variations, but surfaces can be slippery, and some plastic cracks with age. Metal should be rust-resistant.

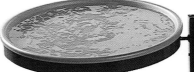

Provide a gradual transition from shallow to deeper water—no more than 3 inches deep. A birdbath might deepen from the edges to the center, or from one end to the other. A bird won't plunge into water of unknown depth but will instead wade in until it finds a level to its liking. If the bath has steep sides, birds may find it difficult to judge the water's depth, so position a flat rock or two in the center.

To allow room for more than one bird at a time, choose a bath that's at least 24 inches in diameter. Smaller birdbaths accommodate single splashers.

To create the necessary traction in slick-bottomed baths, you can add gravel to the bottom—although that does make cleaning more difficult. Lightweight birdbaths need secure pedestals to keep them from being tipped over.

ABOVE: An upside-down iron table base makes a sculptural pedestal for a saucer bath; rocks add visual interest and landing sites.

RIGHT: A plastic saucer in a steel ring mounts either on a wall or post; a three-quarter circle of terra-cotta snugs up to a deck railing.

SAFETY FIRST. A bird wet from bathing can't move as fast as a dry bird, so it's important to place a birdbath close enough to foliage cover that birds can quickly take refuge from predators—but not so close that cats and other marauders can lurk among the shrubs. The space between a ground-level bath and nearby shrubs should be flat and open, giving predators no chance to creep up unnoticed.

A location about 10 to 20 feet from protective shrub cover offers a good safety zone; baths located any farther than that will leave damp birds exposed to hawks and other birds of prey. Avoid sites beneath overhanging tree branches or close to wood fences or flat-topped walls that could serve as launching pads for cats.

BASIC UPKEEP. Keeping the bath filled with clean water is the most important task; an erratic water supply will discourage visitors. If your garden is watered by drip irrigation on an automatic timer, just place an emitter in the birdbath to fill it whenever the watering system operates.

To keep the birdbath inviting, change the water daily during summer and every three or four days in cooler months when the bath is used less often. Use a strong jet from the hose to clean the bowl, and scrub the bottom regularly to remove algae, bacteria, and bird droppings.

If you live where birdbaths freeze over in winter, you'll need to find a way to offer ice-free water in cold weather. The old-fashioned method still works: Use hot water from indoors to melt birdbath ice each morning. Or outfit your birdbath with a small heating element designed especially for birdbaths. The simplest types operate continuously; more expensive models shut off when the temperature reaches a certain level.

TOP: Thanks to a submersible heating element, a robin enjoys a drink in icy weather.

ABOVE: This natural-looking boulder basin is actually fiberglass molded from real rock.

BELOW: A sleek contemporary copper bath on a rusted steel base has a recirculating pump to keep the water moving.

KEEP IT MOVING

Birds especially love water that gently drips or splashes—whether the source is a leaky faucet or an elaborate fountain in a garden pool. Drip-irrigation tubing and emitters make it easy to set up additions to a basic birdbath. You can also purchase mini-misters and drip spouts especially designed to be used in birdbaths or on the ground; they operate directly from a hose or faucet.

Some commercial baths come with built-in fountains, but you can create one yourself by adding a submersible pump and a spray head on a riser. In a natural-looking, ground-level pond,

It may not be elegant, but a dripping faucet satisfies a scrub-jay's thirst.

the same kind of pump can recirculate water in a streambed or waterfall. Pumps should be plugged into outdoor receptacles protected with a ground fault circuit interrupter (GFCI). One type of birdbath fountain operates by means of a small solar panel that powers the submersible pump.

Drippers hooked up to outdoor faucets allow you to add as little as a few drops of water per minute to keep a bath full (many have their own pressure reducers and needle valve controls). Freestanding misters put out a fine spray that will soon have hummingbirds hovering for midair baths. If you don't want to keep the spray going all the time, just turn it on at the same time every day; the birds will soon catch on.

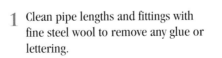

BATHING BEAUTIES

You can customize a birdbath to suit your surroundings—and your aesthetic sensibilities—by making it yourself. The three baths shown on these two pages represent a range of styles, but they all use a simple terra-cotta plant saucer to hold water.

BRANCH BATH

Copper legs sprout branches in this industrial-looking birdbath-cum-sculpture for the garden.

MATERIALS

10 feet of ¾-inch copper pipe, cut with a pipe cutter or hacksaw into three 20-inch pieces, one 12-inch piece, one 1-inch piece, and nine 4-inch pieces (keep the remainder to finish the fourth leg)

Four ¾-inch end caps

Five ¾-inch T-shaped copper pipes

Two ¾-inch 45-degree elbows

Four ¾-inch 90-degree elbows

Slow-setting epoxy adhesive

Twelve ½-inch, #4 sheet metal screws

One terra-cotta saucer, 18 inches in diameter

1 Clean pipe lengths and fittings with fine steel wool to remove any glue or lettering.

2 Test-fit the legs. Three are 20-inch-long pieces with a cap at the bottom and a T at the top; the fourth starts with a cap, the 12-inch pipe, and a sideways T (the branch holder). Cut and add another piece of pipe about 6¼ inches long to make this leg the same length as the others; top with a T. To the branch-holding arm, add the 1-inch length, a 45-degree elbow, a 4-inch piece, and the remaining 45-degree elbow.

3 Test-fit the square ring that supports the saucer, connecting the T atop each leg to two 4-inch pieces of pipe and adding a 90-degree elbow in each corner.

4 Glue the leg pieces together, including the top Ts, applying adhesive to the inside face of each coupling. Let dry for several hours.

5 Glue and connect the remaining top pieces, angling legs outward slightly. Let dry overnight.

6 To reinforce the top, drill holes and insert sheet metal screws into top joints (two into each T and one per elbow). Set saucer on stand, insert a graceful branch, and fill the bath with water.

GLASS AND GROUT BATH

Glass pebbles transform a plain terra-cotta saucer into a sparkling jewel of a birdbath. To make a bigger bath, choose a larger saucer and increase pebble and grout amounts proportionately. Another type of support could be substituted for the bottle legs.

MATERIALS

Waterproof adhesive suitable for glass

About 10 pounds of glass pebbles (from a florists' supply or import store)

One terra-cotta saucer, 16 inches in diameter

Three small green glass bottles

One 5-pound box of green sanded grout

Clear waterproofing sealer

1 Randomly glue glass pebbles on both the inside and outside of the saucer, using small dabs of adhesive. Using a thick bead of glue on the mouth of each bottle, mount bottles to the saucer bottom to create evenly spaced legs. Let dry overnight.

2 Mix grout according to package directions. Dampen saucer with a fine spray of water; beginning with rim and inside of saucer, work grout into spaces between pebbles to about half their depth (wear rubber gloves). Use a damp sponge and a paintbrush to smooth the surface. Turn the saucer upside down and apply grout to outside and bottom.

3 As grout begins to set, smooth and wipe the surfaces with a sponge and a paintbrush. When the surface is hard to the touch, burnish it with a cotton rag.

4 Let the bath dry for a week; then apply three or four coats of sealer. Let the bath dry completely before filling it with water.

TWO-PART BIRDBATH

A birdbath needn't be fancy. This one combines a simple straight-sided terra-cotta pot (10 inches across) with a glazed saucer (16 inches). The saucer rests atop the pot and holds about 3 inches of water. Since this bath stands only about a foot off the ground—easy pouncing distance for a cat—it should be placed in a cleared area, with shrubbery cover within a quick flight's distance.

PONDS AND PUDDLES

Whether you create a small depression out of concrete or engineer something more elaborate, an in-ground watering hole for birds can be a distinctive addition to your backyard landscape.

Options range from pools that you can create from flexible vinyl liners—available in garden centers—to hand-packed concrete or preformed drop-in liners. Be sure to keep pool water shallow, or offer rock landing pads where the water is deeper. Position stones and plants around the edges for a natural look.

Adding a waterfall or fountain will increase your pool's appeal for birds. A simple submersible pump recirculates water through flexible tubing; connect the pump to an outdoor receptacle protected with a GFCI (ground fault circuit interrupter). For a small pond in a sunny location, you could also use a pump powered by a solar panel.

The sound of water from a dripper attracts a Steller's jay to a sunken bath assembled from a kit. Rocks from a building supply yard anchor the 3- by 5-foot synthetic rubber pond liner.

BAMBOO WATERSPOUT

This traditional waterspout—*tsukubai* in Japanese—is a simple way to provide running water for birds. Team up this spout with the concrete puddle shown opposite, or use a rock with a natural hollow or other small collecting basin.

It's easy to hollow out bamboo for use as piping: Just ram in a metal rod to puncture the joints, then run flexible tubing through and connect the tubing to a drip system or faucet. Set the water flow at a very slow trickle, channeling any overflow to irrigate nearby plants or run into a larger pond.

To conserve moisture, hook up the system to a tiny pump on a timer or turn on a ball valve at certain times of the day.

Puncture bamboo joints

Plastic tubing

Pump

KEEP WARM: TAKE A BATH

It's easy to understand the attraction of water for cooling off in hot weather, but birds benefit by taking baths in winter, too. Bathing during cold weather actually helps insulate birds by keeping their feathers free of dirt and leaving space for pockets of air—except when it's so cold that water would freeze on the birds' wings.

PUDDLE OF CONCRETE

What could look more natural in a birdscape than a puddle? This one is permanent—you create a form to shape it, then move it into place for the birds.

1 Tape a 7-foot length of 6-inch aluminum flashing into a loop and lay it on flat ground, edge up, in a free-form pond shape. Using a few stakes to hold the flashing in place, line the inside with a shallow layer of sand (a quart or so); curve the sand up along the edges.

2 Mix 60 pounds of ready-mix fiberglass-reinforced concrete with about a gallon of water (don't make it soupy). Wear rubber gloves to hand-pack the concrete into the form you've created, building up the sides to create a shallow bowl. Use a 2- to 3-inch scraper blade to round over the top edges.

3 Let the concrete dry overnight, then remove flashing.

4 If you wish, stain the cured concrete brown (as in photo) by giving it a coat of diluted liquid iron fertilizer: 4 parts water to 1 part fertilizer.

5 Seal the concrete with several coats of clear waterproofing sealer, then dust with sand while it's still wet to give the surface a beach texture.

6 Form a depression in the ground where you want to position your puddle, set the puddle in place, and fill it with water.

Whether plain or fanciful, nest boxes need to have the right dimensions and hole size for the species you're trying to attract—like the Carolina chickadee above.

NESTING STRUCTURES

Birds can suffer from a housing shortage, especially in developed areas where natural vegetation has been removed and gardens aren't mature enough to provide desirable nesting sites. Even rural farmland may not be hospitable; as woods are cut, brush is cleared, and tree crops are tended, the number of good nesting areas is reduced. Man-made nesting structures can provide a remedy—and lure birds into your garden.

Only cavity-nesting birds (those that nest in holes in trees) use birdhouses; these include chickadees, nuthatches, wrens, bluebirds, and some swallows, among other backyard birds. To accommodate species that don't nest in cavities, such as barn swallows, robins, and phoebes, you can put up nesting shelves. These open-sided structures offer a bonus—they let you observe the activities of your tenants.

All birdhouses aren't created equal, and different kinds of houses appeal to different birds. House dimensions, size of the entrance hole, and mounting height need to be tailored to the particular species you're trying to attract. (For guidelines, see the chart on page 43 and refer to the species descriptions in "A Garden Guest List," pages 85–125.) These aren't hard-and-fast rules, but your odds of attracting tenants will be improved if you come close to following them. Remember that even though a birdhouse may be designed for a wren, chickadee, or bluebird, it will be fair game for any bird of similar size.

Tree swallows may choose creative nest sites—like this gate pipe.

Nowadays you'll find an abundance of decorative birdhouses representing a range of materials and artistic fancies. Such houses make fine garden art, but they may not work as living spaces for birds. Most functional nesting boxes are made to handle all sorts of weather, and they're usually unpainted—birds tend to shy away from the cute, colorful houses that attract humans.

Whether you're buying or building, wood is the old standby and has good insulating properties—but you can also find birdhouses made of ceramic, metal, acrylic, PVC pipe, gourd, and other materials. Aluminum purple martin houses are popular and easier to hoist than wood.

Different bird species nest at different heights. For best success, mount boxes at the preferred height of the birds you hope to host.

LOCATION, LOCATION, LOCATION

In bird real estate, like any other, location is everything. Know the kinds of birds that frequent your locale, and tailor your accommodations to their habitat preferences.

Keep birdhouses away from feeders—mealtime bustle makes nesting birds nervous. If you put up more than one nest box, it's best to keep houses well separated and out of sight of one another—nesting birds like privacy. A gallery of houses can be decorative, but it probably won't attract more than one nesting pair.

Face house entrances away from prevailing weather. To keep nest boxes safe from raccoons and cats, mount them on metal poles. If you want to put a birdhouse in a tree, hang it from a branch that is partially protected from the elements and the watchful eyes of predators.

SOME BIRDHOUSE BASICS

Make sure your houses are installed in plenty of time for the nesting season. Migrant birds start returning in some areas as early as February and look for nest sites soon after they arrive. Keep the following pointers in mind:

- ∾ Remove any perch your birdhouse was supplied with—it's unnecessary, and house sparrows may use it to heckle birds inside.

- ∾ Birdhouses should be made from materials that insulate well, like wood that's at least ¾-inch thick.

- ∾ One side or the top should open for cleaning (before the next nesters arrive) and monitoring the nest box, and there should be drain holes on the bottom and ventilation holes high up on the sides.

- ∾ Add a textured surface on the inside wall below the entry, to allow hatchlings to climb to the hole.

- ∾ Angle the roof and extend it well beyond the entry, both to keep rainwater out and to discourage predators. Double-thick entry holes help keep predators such as raccoons from reaching in.

- ∾ If you hang a birdhouse, keep the chain short to minimize swinging.

Once birds are nesting—like these barn swallows—they shouldn't be disturbed.

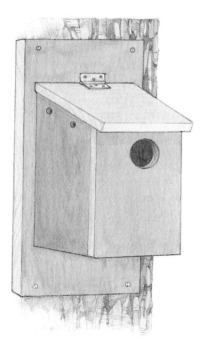

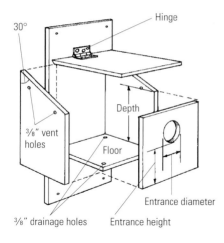

30°

Hinge

⅜" vent holes

Depth

Floor

Entrance diameter

⅜" drainage holes

Entrance height

PREDATOR BLOCKS

You can make it harder for outsiders to harrass the occupants of your birdhouse by adding a predator block—a piece that makes the entrance hole extra deep. Simply screw a scrap block of wood to the inside of the front as shown in the diagram on the facing page. Drill through both the house front and the block at once, using a power drill with hole saw or spade bit.

Ready-to-install predator guards of wood or plastic are also available at bird supply stores.

BASIC BIRDHOUSE

If you have even a passing acquaintance with a hammer and nails, you should be able to fashion a basic birdhouse like the one shown on this page, designed with a hinged roof for seasonal cleaning access. The model on the facing page, featuring a pivoting front, has slightly more advanced construction details. Alter these designs or mix and match features as you wish.

Base your measurements on the kind of birds you want to accommodate, as shown on the chart on page 43. Use any 1-by (¾-inch) or scrap lumber (decay-resistant woods such as redwood, cedar, and cypress are best).

For ease of attachment, the hinged-roof house needs an extended back wall unless you are mounting it on a pole. The backing board is optional for the version on the next page, since the swinging door makes it easier to attach through the back.

Rip (cut to width) and crosscut (cut to length) the pieces and cut roof bevels with a handsaw, portable circular saw, saber saw, or—faster and more accurate—a table saw. Drill the entrance hole with a power drill and spade bit or hole saw. The bevel (angle cut) where roof meets backing board on the hinged-roof house makes the joint more seaworthy, but it's not absolutely essential.

If you want to fashion a drip cap on the roof piece, as shown in the diagram on the facing page, cut a groove with the dado blade of a table saw or use a portable router and straight bit. To make a climbing surface for young birds, as shown in the top photo, cut ⅛-inch-deep horizontal grooves at ½-inch intervals on the inside of the front below the entrance hole.

Join pieces with galvanized box nails, finishing nails (countersink them with a nailset), or decking screws (drive them with a power drill and Phillips-head screwdriver bit).

To form the pivot points for the front of the house with the swinging-door, drill through each side wall into the edge of the front piece, about 1 inch from the top; then tap in ⅜-inch dowels. Sand the dowels flush, but don't glue them. Secure the front with a locking pin or screw, as shown in the diagram on the facing page.

If you prefer, the front can swing open from the bottom, as in the photo at top; position the dowel pivots 1 inch from the bottom, making sure the door will clear the roof overhang. To hold the front in place, drill a hole for a nail at a downward angle through each side into the door edge.

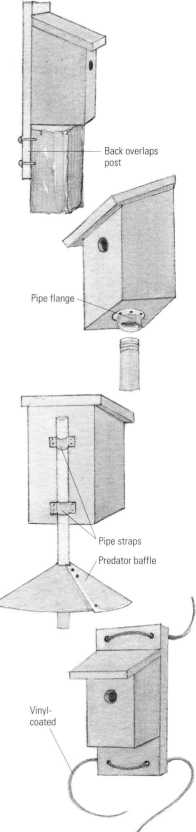

Back overlaps post

Pipe flange

Pipe straps

Predator baffle

Vinyl-coated

Horizontal grooves on the inside of the front serve as a ladder for fledglings to reach the hole.

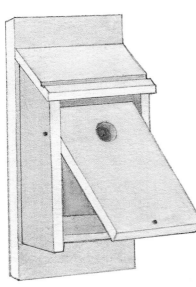

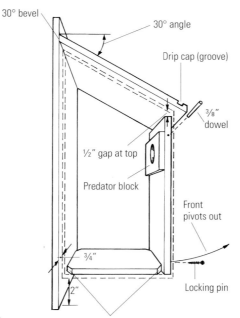

30° bevel

30° angle

Drip cap (groove)

3/8" dowel

1/2" gap at top

Predator block

Front pivots out

3/4"

2"

Locking pin

Notch corners for drainage

A mountain bluebird finds a home.

ON THE BLUEBIRD TRAIL

Over the past century, bluebirds lost much of their nesting habitats across North America to urban sprawl and to aggressive competition from house sparrows and European starlings, both imports from Europe.

In 1978 the North American Bluebird Society was formed, and its efforts have contributed greatly toward reversing the decline of the bluebird population. Now the society is establishing a Transcontinental Bluebird Trail of bluebird nesting boxes all across the United States and Canada.

Volunteers build houses especially designed for these birds, locating the boxes in appropriate habitats and monitoring them to protect the birds from danger.

Specifications for the boxes differ somewhat for different bluebird species and geographical regions. To find out what's best in your area, contact your local branch of the North American Bluebird Society or visit the society's website (www.nabluebirdsociety.org).

The house can be customized however you wish, as in these variations (from left): shingle roof, stucco-patch siding with painted vine, and grooved door with pebble "handle"; diagonal lattice; eucalyptus bark nailed and glued on in layers.

NESTING SHELVES

Certain bird species—robins, phoebes, and barn swallows are good examples—prefer to nest on open platforms rather than in standard "box" houses. You can accommodate them by building one of these nesting shelves.

The two platforms are easy to build from any surfaced 1-by lumber. Cut pieces to allow for the floor space and depth indicated on page 43, using a compass saw or jigsaw for the curved pieces. Drill drainage holes in the floor, and nail pieces together.

These units were designed to hang just below eaves or high on a wall somewhat protected from the elements—and from the eyes of predators. Robins are also fond of "hidden" nooks in ivy or other vines. Drill two slots near the top of the back wall of the assembled shelf, then slip the slots over nails or screws secured to house siding.

BARN SWALLOW SHELF

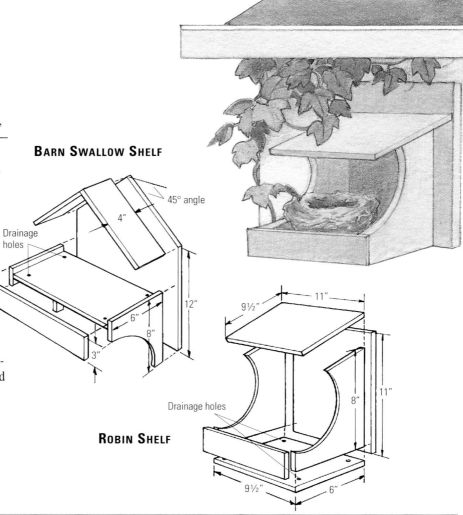

ROBIN SHELF

A Carolina wren collects moss to build a nest.

FEATHERING THEIR NESTS

Birds collect all sorts of materials for constructing and lining their nests. You can help them out—and increase the chances they'll nest in your yard—by offering supplies.

Try putting out lint from your clothes dryer (don't use fabric softener), strands of yarn or string, hair from family pets or your own hairbrush, thin strips of cloth, down from an old pillow or garment, packing excelsior, dried grasses, or pine needles. You can also buy nesting materials at bird supply stores. Yarn and string pieces shouldn't be longer than 5 or 6 inches.

Begin offering materials in early spring for the first nest-builders. Place these in a basket, box, or suet feeder hung from a tree limb or set out in an easily spotted location. Yarn or string can also be arranged on shrubs. Use the same container and location each time so that birds will know where to look.

As the season progresses, you may be able to track your backyard visitors by spotting your nesting materials in trees, shrubs, and nest boxes throughout the neighborhood.

Wren house

Chickadee
house

Bluebird house

SPECIES	FLOOR OF CAVITY	DEPTH (FLOOR TO ROOF)	ENTRANCE ABOVE FLOOR	DIAM. OF ENTR.	HEIGHT ABOVE GROUND
House wren	4" × 4"	6"–8"	4"–6"	1"–1½"	6'–10'
Carolina wren	4" × 4"	6"–8"	4"–6"	1"–1½"	6'–10'
Black-capped chickadee	4" × 4"	8"–10"	6"–8"	1⅛"	6'–15'
Tufted titmouse	4" × 4"	8"–10"	6"–8"	1¼"	6'–15'
Nuthatch	4" × 4"	8"–10"	6"–8"	1¼"	12'–20'
Bluebird	5" × 5"	8"	6"	1½"	5'–10'
House finch*	6" × 6"	6"	4"	2"	8'–12'
Robin	6" × 8"	8"	N/A	N/A	6'–15'
Black or eastern phoebe	6" × 6"	6"	N/A	N/A	8'
Violet-green swallow	5" × 5"	6"–8"	4"–6"	1"–1½"; or ⅞" x 2"	10'–15'
Tree swallow	5" × 5"	6"–8"	4"–6"	1"–1½"	10'–15'
Barn swallow	6" × 6"	6"	N/A	N/A	8'–12'
Purple martin	6" × 6"	6"	1"	2½"	15'–20'
Downy woodpecker	4" × 4"	8"–10"	6"–8"	1¼"	6'–20'
Hairy woodpecker	6" × 6"	12"–15"	9"–12"	1½"	12'–20'
Northern flicker	7" × 7"	16"–18"	14"–16"	2½"	6'–20'
Red-headed woodpecker	6" × 6"	12"–15"	9"–12"	2"	12'–20'
Screech-owl	8" × 8"	12"–15"	9"–12"	3"	10'–30'

*House finches may use open platforms.

THE RIGHT HOUSE FOR THE RIGHT BIRD

Before you buy a birdhouse or pick up a hammer and nails to build one, become acquainted with some basic bird "building codes." Different species require different accommodations, so the kind of house you install determines the kinds of birds you're likely to attract. A shoebox-size house with a 2-inch entrance hole won't tempt passing wrens, for example. They'll find it too big to be cozy, and the opening will let larger birds enter and threaten them.

The chart at left lists the general needs of a variety of backyard birds—what floor dimensions and floor-to-ceiling depth they generally prefer, how big the entrance hole should be, and how far up the entry should be from the floor. The chart also shows how high aboveground you should mount the house to make it appealing.

Screech-owl house

Purple martins may set up housekeeping in multi-storied apartment houses or in gourd communities.

WHO INVITED *YOU?*

You can't be sure the tenants you think you're inviting will actually be the birds to inhabit your nesting boxes. But you can take steps to improve the odds.

- If you want violet-green swallows but not house sparrows, make an oblong entrance hole $7/8$ inch high by 2 inches wide. Swallows can squeeze through but house sparrows cannot.

- Tree swallows often take over bluebird houses. Some people mount two bluebird houses on adjacent posts so that swallows will take one, then fight off swallows that try to take the other, leaving it open for bluebirds.

- To keep house sparrows from evicting chickadees or other small birds, make the entrance hole $1 1/8$ inches across—too small to let the house sparrows in.

- Fill a flicker box with wood chips. This is inviting material for the flickers to excavate but not appealing to other birds.

- Paint the inside of purple martin houses white to deter starlings from taking them over.

PURPLE MARTIN APARTMENT

Purple martins are among the few birds that like to congregate with their relatives in an apartment-style dwelling. The structure should be light enough that it's easy to raise and lower for cleaning, and it must have good ventilation—purple martins take up residence for the whole hot summer.

The house shown at right is built from $1/2$-inch exterior plywood, with asphalt composition shingles nailed to the roof. A horizontal "ventilation shaft" on each floor improves air circulation on warm summer days, as does the air space beneath the roof. As your house catches on, you can easily expand upward—the design is modular.

Nail each story together independently, filling any edge gaps in the plywood with wood putty and sanding them smooth. Paint the building inside and out with white exterior latex to keep it cooler. Fasten one floor to the next with hooks and eyes, and then mount the assembled structure on a stout pole or post.

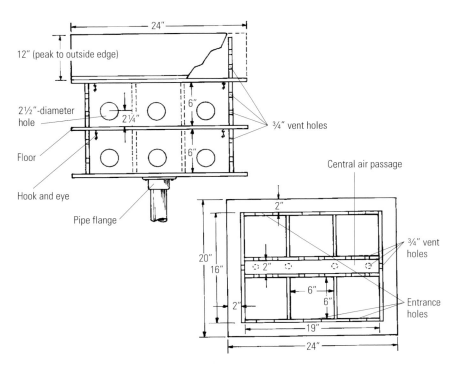

PREDATORS AND PESTS

When backyard feeders begin to attract lots of birds, pests and predators are likely to show up, too. You can take benign steps to reduce a predator's advantage and to discourage pests from devouring the food you're putting out for the birds.

CATS. For the best protection, attach a small bell to your cat's collar to warn birds of its approach. Cyclone fencing around your yard, if secure at buildings and gates and flush with the ground, will keep neighborhood cats out. Remove such means of access as overhanging tree branches. When cats do come around, discourage them with loud noise or a squirt from a water pistol.

Low fencing can help in the immediate vicinity of ground-feeding birds. Cats will have to jump over it, giving birds just enough warning to escape.

Locate low feeders and birdbaths within 20 feet of cover but a safe distance of 10 feet or so from shrubbery where crouching cats could hide. Thorny shrubs can be closer—they keep cats out. Raise feeders on slippery 6-foot metal poles for maximum protection against both cats and raccoons.

HAWKS. Place feeders close enough to dense cover that birds can quickly flee to safety. If the threat continues, restrict feeding to early morning so that birds will have dispersed before the hawks are up and about.

SQUIRRELS. Frequent and inventive invaders of feeders, squirrels can sometimes be deflected by providing them with their own feeding station. Offer them peanuts, corn, and sunflower seeds —if you don't mind possibly attracting all their relatives, too.

You can buy baffles to attach underneath pole-mounted feeders and over hanging ones to discourage squirrels as well as raccoons and rats. Even so, a feeder needs to be a good distance from a tree or fence to be out of a leaping squirrel's reach. Backyard birders have also had some success with these methods:

∾ Hang the feeder by heavy monofilament fishing line, which is difficult for a squirrel to navigate.

∾ Suspend the feeder from a clothesline between pulleys, encasing the line with 2-inch plastic pipe segments that will spin when a squirrel steps on them.

∾ Feed early in the day, and don't put out too much seed. Birds will tend to clean out the feeder quickly, leaving nothing for squirrels.

AGGRESSIVE BIRDS. Pigeons, jays, starlings, house sparrows, and blackbirds sometimes dominate bird feeders, keeping smaller birds away. The best way to deflect unwelcome bird species is simply to eliminate the kind of food that attracts them. Reduce the total amount of food you put out and provide only small openings and perches on feeders.

To discourage pigeons, eliminate cracked corn, chicken scratch, grains, and bread crumbs; keep the ground under feeders clean. To make feeders less attractive to house sparrows, it may help to stop providing millet. If jays become a bother, try giving them their own feeding station a good distance from other feeders, offering peanuts, other nutmeats, and sunflower seeds.

If blackbirds and starlings encroach en masse, the only solution may be to temporarily stop all supplemental feeding. When you begin anew, put out limited portions in small feeders.

Northern cardinals easily partake of the seed in this hopper feeder, but its spring-weighted perches can be adjusted so that they won't hold heavier birds—or thieving squirrels.

Once you have a general plan in mind, turning your yard into a real bird habitat comes down to a thoughtful selection of specific plants. With the right mix of trees, shrubs, and

BIRDSCAPING,
PLANT
BY
PLANT

vines, along with annual and perennial flowers and even grasses, you will be able to meet the needs of many different species of birds.

Choosing plants for birds goes a step beyond simply selecting plants as part of a garden design. Attractive form and foliage aren't enough—you want your plants to help provide for the birds' needs for food and shelter. Food might mean berries, seeds, nuts, or nectar from blossoms—or it might mean the insects that are attracted to a planting. Shelter could be evergreen boughs that provide a buffer from the elements in winter, a hidden branch where a nest can be constructed, or a thorny tangle that makes a convenient sanctuary from predators.

To appeal to a wide range of bird species, aim for as much diversity of plant material as your garden can encompass. Keep in mind that your neighbors' plants can contribute to the general scheme of things, too—from the birds' standpoint, it's all one big backyard.

If you make the right plant choices, birds will find your garden. The tangy fruit of this crabapple tree *(Malus)* provides satisfying sustenance for a cedar waxwing.

GARDENING BY THE MAP

Yucca aloifolia

WHAT'S A NATIVE?

You'll see the term "native plant" as you search for good plants for your birdscape. Just what does it mean?

A native plant is one that's indigenous to a place—as opposed to one that has been introduced (an "exotic"), even if that plant has become a familiar part of the landscape.

By itself, "native" doesn't mean anything. It needs qualifying words to tell you where it's native (California native, for example). What's native in one part of the country isn't necessarily native in another region.

When you choose plants native to your geographic area, you know they're suited to your climate—and will provide familiar food and shelter for native birds and regular migrants. Some nurseries have native plant sections, usually offering plants native to that state.

Sassafras albidum

Birds abound in every part of the North American continent where gardeners can grow plants. But the bird population differs from one region to another—and so does the selection of plants that will thrive there.

The trees, shrubs, and vines described in the following pages are all known to attract birds—and they are all likely to improve the look of your garden. To help you choose the ones that are best suited to your particular area, we've divided the United States into six broad climatic regions as shown on the map below. Throughout this chapter, plant entries are color-coded to show you at a glance which plants are likely to perform well in your region.

This brief encyclopedia of plants is a good starting point. Of course, there are many other trees, shrubs, and vines that might be useful in your locale. Native plants of any region include bird-enticing species that grow almost solely within the confines of their native territory; a well-stocked nursery that deals in natives can enrich your range of choices. If you live in a desert or mountain area, you're probably especially aware of the importance of native plants. They're the ones you can count on to be suited to the climate—and to appeal to the local wildlife.

To glean further suggestions of plants or species that thrive in your area, visit regional arboreta and botanic gardens, ask at your nursery, or check a reliable garden guide covering your region. The local Audubon Society chapter also may be able to suggest plants that are known to be bird favorites where you live.

- ● NORTHERN PACIFIC COAST
- ○ SOUTHERN PACIFIC COAST, LOW DESERT
- ● MOUNTAINS, GREAT BASIN, HIGH DESERT
- ● PLAINS AND PRAIRIES
- ● SOUTHEAST
- ○ NORTHEAST

USING THE LISTINGS

To quickly determine if a particular tree, shrub, or vine might be appropriate for your garden, look at the color coding at the top of the entry for the plant. A color dot that matches the map color for your part of the country means the plant is suited to your general climate. If certain species grow better there than others, those species are recommended at the end of the entry. If no species are called out even though the plant is suited to your region, you can freely choose among available species—all should do well in your climate.

Of course, each of the broad climate regions on the map encompasses great variations in conditions. To be sure that a particular plant can be expected to thrive in your own "microclimate," ask at a local nursery.

Plants are listed according to their botanical names, followed by their common names and these symbols:

🌿 tells you the plant is evergreen; it keeps its foliage all year.

🌳 means it's deciduous, with foliage that will drop off and be replaced the following growing season with new foliage. Some plant entries include both evergreen and deciduous species.

☼, ●, or ◐ shows the plant's general exposure needs—for sun, shade, or either partial shade (shade for part of the day) or light shade (filtered or indirect sunlight). A few plants are adaptable to such a wide range of conditions that both sun and shade are shown.

➤ indicates the plant's particular value to birds—for shelter, for the food it produces (berries, seeds, and so on), or for the insects it draws.

Berberis thunbergii

CAUTION: PLANT INVADERS!

Some of the birds' favorite plants are likely to become colonizers when birds consume and spread their berries and seeds. In your garden, these will appear as volunteer seedlings—welcome if you need more plants. But some plants, under optimum conditions, will volunteer in uncultivated countryside—and when these plants differ from the native flora, they can crowd out the natives. This jeopardizes both the native plants and the wildlife that depends on them.

The following list contains plants known to be aggressive colonizers of wild territory in some parts of North America. Before choosing one of these, check with a reputable local nursery or your county's Cooperative Extension Office to make sure that it doesn't present an invasion problem in your region.

Albizia julibrissin (mimosa, silk tree)
Ampelopsis brevipedunculata (porcelain berry)
Berberis thunbergii (Japanese barberry)
Brussonetia papyrifera (paper mulberry)
Celastrus orbiculatus (Asiatic bittersweet)
Cotoneaster
Elaeagnus, some species
Euonymus alatus (burning bush)
Ficus carica (edible fig)
Ligustrum (privet), some species
Lonicera (honeysuckle), some species
Melia azedarach (chinaberry tree)
Morus alba (white mulberry)
Nandina domestica (heavenly bamboo)
Pennisetum setaceum (fountain grass)
Phalaris arundinacea (ribbon grass)
Pyracantha (firethorn)
Rhamnus (buckthorn), some species
Rosa multiflora (multiflora rose)
Sapium sebiferum (Chinese tallow tree)

TREES

Birds rely on trees both for food and for shelter. Trees supply varied dietary needs: seeds, flowers, fruit, insects. Shelter means nest sites—on branches or in trunk cavities—as well as protective cover from predators and from rain, snow, and winter chill. Where winter temperatures drop to zero or below, needle-leafed evergreen trees provide a critical shield against the elements.

On these pages you'll find descriptions of many trees that are favorites of birds and make attractive and adaptable additions to home landscapes. Large shade trees provide a canopy, while shorter trees create an understory. The combination—whether it's entirely in your yard or overlapping into neighboring gardens—will appeal to a variety of birds by simulating a woodland edge. See page 71 for a separate listing of trees to attract hummingbirds and page 53 for trees that have particular value to birds in desert areas.

Liquidambar styraciflua

Abies nordmanniana

Acer ginnala

ABIES
🌲 FIR
● ● ● CLIMATE REGIONS
☼ SUN
↘ SEEDS, INSECTS, SHELTER

Thick canopies of foliage provide good shelter, especially welcome in snowy winter, and many birds relish the seeds scattered when cones ripen in spring and summer. Firs prefer a cool, moist atmosphere and clean air; they grow best in northern states or mountainous areas.

🌲 EVERGREEN 🌲 DECIDUOUS
● NORTHERN PACIFIC COAST
● SOUTHERN PACIFIC COAST, LOW DESERT
● MOUNTAINS, GREAT BASIN, HIGH DESERT
● PLAINS AND PRAIRIES
● SOUTHEAST ● NORTHEAST
↘ VALUE TO BIRDS

Trees are spirelike and can reach 50 to 100 feet or more in the garden, depending on the species; most prefer acid soil, well drained.

RECOMMENDED:
● *A. amabilis, A. concolor, A. nordmanniana, A. procera*
● *A. concolor, A. grandis, A. lasiocarpa*
● *A. balsamea, A. concolor, A. homolepis*

ACER
🌲 MAPLE
● ● ● ● ● CLIMATE REGIONS
☼ ☼ SUN, PARTIAL SHADE
↘ BUDS, SEEDS, SHELTER

Nearly all maples have dense, sheltering foliage, and all bear seeds (ripening in late summer or early fall) in winged papery casings. There are maples for nearly all climates, in a range of sizes and shapes. Virtually all exhibit colorful fall foliage in yellow, orange, or red. Most have extensive, shallow root systems that need regular moisture; to hold their own against maple roots, the best nearby plantings are vigorous shrubs, ground covers, or lawn.

RECOMMENDED:
● *A. campestre, A. cappadocicum 'Rubrum', A. ginnala, A. glabrum, A. negundo, A. tataricum*
● *A. ginnala, A. negundo*

ALNUS
🌲 ALDER
● ● ● CLIMATE REGIONS
☼ ☼ SUN, LIGHT SHADE
↘ SEEDS, POLLEN, SHELTER

In winter, hanging seed catkins attract a variety of birds. In the growing season, insects feed various songbirds; sapsuckers mine trunks. Fast-growing (some species to 90 feet), alders show kinship to birches in smooth trunks and foliage crowns that are usually taller than they are wide. They grow best with regular moisture and are attractive in groves. Fall foliage color is yellow to rusty brown.

RECOMMENDED:
- ● *A. cordata, A. glutinosa, A. oregona, A. rhombifolia*
- ○ *A. cordata, A. glutinosa, A. rhombifolia;* not grown in desert
- ● *A. glutinosa, A. tenuifolia*

Alnus tenuifolia

AMELANCHIER
❦ SERVICEBERRY, SHADBLOW
   ● ● ○ CLIMATE REGIONS
   ☼ SUN
   ➤ FRUIT

Most serviceberries are shrubby (see page 58), but three species—*A. arborea, A. canadensis,* and *A. laevis*—become graceful, lightweight, small to medium-size trees. Showy clusters of white or pinkish flowers in early spring precede leaves. By summer, small dark blue berries attract many birds. Foliage turns red or yellow in autumn.

RECOMMENDED:
- ●● *A. canadensis, A. laevis*

Amelanchier canadensis

BETULA
❦ BIRCH
   ● ● ● ● ○ CLIMATE REGIONS
   ☼ ◑ SUN, PARTIAL SHADE
   ➤ BUDS, SEEDS, INSECTS

Birches lure birds with seed catkins hanging from bare winter branches. During growing season, plentiful insects are an added attraction. Familiar sights in northern and high-altitude regions, birches also include species that adapt to more temperate lowland gardens. These tall trees prefer regular moisture and have somewhat competitive roots near the surface. Foliage turns bright yellow in fall.

RECOMMENDED:
- ●● *B. pendula*
- ○ *B. pendula;* not grown in desert
- ● *B. papyrifera*
- ● *B. lenta, B. papyrifera, B. populifolia*

Betula papyrifera

Carpinus betulus

Celtis occidentalis

CARPINUS
❦ HORNBEAM
   ● ● ● CLIMATE REGIONS
   ☼ ◑ SUN, LIGHT SHADE
   ➤ FRUIT, SHELTER

Hanging clusters of nutlike fruits provide food in autumn. Pyramidal to round-headed, these medium-size trees look neat all year. Dense, dark foliage turns brilliant yellow to red in fall.

RECOMMENDED:
- ● *C. betulus, C. caroliniana*
- ●● *C. caroliniana*

CELTIS
❦ HACKBERRY
   ● ● ● ● CLIMATE REGIONS
   ☼ ◑ SUN, LIGHT SHADE
   ➤ FRUIT, SHELTER

Besides providing small clusters of berrylike fruits in fall, hackberries offer the shade and grace of elms—without the disease problem that makes elms risky. Deep-rooted, these tall trees won't crack pavement or compete with nearby plants. Most species leaf out late in spring, turning bright yellow in autumn.

RECOMMENDED:
- ○ *C. australis, C. occidentalis, C. sinensis*
- ●● *C. occidentalis, C. reticulata*
- ● *C. laevigata*

CORNUS
❦ DOGWOOD
   ● ● ● CLIMATE REGIONS
   ☼ ◑ SUN, PARTIAL SHADE
   ➤ FRUIT, INSECTS, SHELTER

Gardeners prize dogwood trees for their spring flowers (actually showy bracts surrounding tiny flowers); birds relish the fruits that follow. An insect population adds appeal. The shrub-tree *C. alternifolia* lacks showy flowers but has plenty of fruit. Flowering dogwood *(C. florida)* is the most widely planted—a medium-size tree with flower bracts in white,

WHAT'S SEX GOT TO DO WITH IT?

Many plants produce small berries that are favorite foods for various birds. With some plants—cotoneaster and pyracantha, for example—the process is simple: You plant it, it produces flowers and fruits, then the birds come to it. But with certain other berry-bearing plants—such as juniper and most hollies—you can't automatically expect fruits. That's because male and female flowers are produced on separate plants. Only the female plants yield berries and then only if there's a male plant nearby for pollination.

How do you determine the sex of a plant? You can't, unless you see berries—which tells you that plant is female. For plants that are valued for ornamental fruits (such as holly), you can buy named selections known to be female or male. This guarantees fruit on the females, provided that you grow a male for pollination (or have one in your immediate neighborhood). Some growers even graft a branch of a male plant onto a female so that you only need one plant.

But in many cases—juniper is a prime example—named individuals have been selected solely for their growth habits; fruiting isn't a consideration. And in other cases, such as spicebush (*Lindera*), there has been no selection of named forms.

When shopping for separate-sex plants, check to see if there are named selections that are specifically fruit- or pollen-producing. Lacking that, shop during the fruiting season and look for berries. Buy one or more plants with fruits and also buy a fruitless one, on the assumption that it may be male. Without berries to guide you, you can only take potluck and set out multiple plants, hoping that you will have both a female and a male in the mix.

pink, or nearly red. Larger trees, *C. controversa* and *C. nuttallii*, grow to 50 feet or more. All are especially attractive against taller evergreens. Autumn foliage can be yellow to red.

RECOMMENDED:
- *C. controversa, C. florida, C. nuttallii*
- *C. alternifolia, C. florida*

Cornus florida with white-throated sparrow

Crataegus phaenopyrum

Elaeagnus angustifolia

Ilex aquifolium

CRATAEGUS
❀ HAWTHORN
- ● ● ● ● ● CLIMATE REGIONS
- ☼ SUN
- ➤ FRUIT, INSECTS, SHELTER

These small to medium-size trees offer colorful flowers, decorative fruits relished by many birds, and colorful autumn foliage. Aphids may be another bird lure during the growing season. Most hawthorns are dense and armed with sharp thorns. Typically, white flowers appear after spring leaf-out; clustered red fruits (like tiny apples) ripen in summer or autumn. Double-flowered selections generally produce no fruit.

RECOMMENDED:
- ● ● ● *C. crus-galli, C. laevigata, C. phaenopyrum*
- ● *C. crus-galli, C. laevigata, C. lavallei, C. phaenopyrum*
- ● *C. succulenta, C. 'Toba'*

ELAEAGNUS angustifolia
❀ RUSSIAN OLIVE
- ● ● ● CLIMATE REGIONS
- ☼ SUN
- ➤ FRUIT, SHELTER

After inconspicuous fragrant flowers in early summer comes a treat for birds—olivelike, silvery yellow fruits. Silvery gray foliage and a graceful appearance mask a tough constitution. Fast-growing to 35 feet, this small tree thrives even in poor, dry soil, summer heat, and winter cold.

ILEX
❀ ❀ HOLLY
- ● ● ● CLIMATE REGIONS
- ☼ ◑ SUN, PARTIAL SHADE
- ➤ FRUIT, SHELTER

Dense foliage gives shelter, and berries provide food to many birds. Evergreen species with spiny leaves are valued as year-round safe havens. Although hollies are shrubby plants (see page 60), several species eventually develop into small to

Continued on page 54 >

A DESERT BIRDSCAPE

A host of migrant bird species as well as year-round residents are potential visitors to desert gardens. If you select the right plants, your landscape can prosper with little or no water, attracting birds with fruits, seeds, and flowers.

Many bird species seek refuge in the branches and foliage of desert plants, sparse though these may appear. Even cacti can be useful, both for their blossoms and for the spines that can protect nests from predators.

Black-chinned hummingbird visits claret cup cactus.

The plants listed below can thrive in the desert—and benefit birds. By virtue of size, such desert signature plants as saguaro cactus have been grouped with trees.

Chilopsis linearis

TREES

Carnegiea gigantea (saguaro)
Celtis reticulata (western hackberry)
Cercidium (palo verde)
Chilopsis linearis (desert willow)*
Fouquieria splendens (ocotillo)*
Fraxinus velutina (Arizona ash)
Juniperus occidentalis
   (western juniper)
Leucaena (leadtree)
Olneya tesota (desert ironwood)
Parkinsonia aculeata
   (Mexican palo verde)
Pinus (pine)
Populus fremontii
   (western cottonwood)
Quercus (oak)
Rhus (sumac)
Yucca, all species

SHRUBS AND VINES

Atriplex (saltbush), several species
Baccharis 'Centennial'
Berberis haematocarpa
   (red barberry)
Buddleia (butterfly bush)*
Choisya dumosa
   (starleaf Mexican orange)
Cordia parvifolia (littleleaf cordia)
Encelia farinosa (brittle bush)
Garrya fremontii
   (Fremont silktassel)
Hyptis emori (desert lavender)
Parthenocissus inserta
   (Virginia creeper)
Prosopis (mesquite)
Rhamnus (buckthorn), several
   species
Rhus ovata (sugar bush)
Salix exigua (desert willow)
Sambucus mexicana
   (blue elderberry)
Trichostema lanatum
   (woolly blue curls)*
Vitis arizonica (canyon grape)
Vitis girdiana (desert wild grape)

** These plants are hummingbird
   favorites.*

ANNUALS AND PERENNIALS

Calliandra eriophylla
   (fairy duster, mesquitilla)
Coreopsis
Echinocereus triglochidiatus
   (claret cup cactus)
Encelia californica (coast sunflower)
Ephedra trifurca (Mormon tea)
Erigeron divergens (fleabane)
Erigonum (wild buckwheat), some
   species*
Eschscholzia californica
   (California poppy)
Hesperaloe parviflora*
Justicia californica (chuparosa)*
Opuntia basilaris (beaver tail)
Opuntia fulgida (jumping cactus)
Penstemon*
Salvia*
Verbascum (mullein)
Zauschneria californica
   (California fuchsia)*

Hesperaloe parviflora

medium-size trees. Most bear male and female flowers on separate plants; for a female holly to produce berries, you need a male plant nearby, flowering at the same time. Provide good soil and regular moisture; hollies will thrive in partial shade, but you'll get more berries in full sun.

RECOMMENDED:
- I. aquifolium, I. latifolia, I. opaca
- I. aquifolium, I. cassine, I. decidua, I. opaca
- I. decidua, I. opaca

JUNIPERUS
❈ JUNIPER
●●●●●● CLIMATE REGIONS
☼ SUN
↘ FRUIT, SHELTER

Some birds eat juniper berries, and many more welcome the evergreen winter shelter. Male and female flowers are usually borne on separate plants; to be sure a plant will bear fruit, buy when berries are present. Dense growth can contain both needlelike or spiny juvenile leaves and scalelike mature foliage—green, steel blue, gray, or red-tinted in winter. Strongly upright, juniper trees are fairly slow growing, reaching 20 to 60 feet depending on the species. They're drought-resistant and tolerate a variety of soils.

RECOMMENDED:
- J. deppeana, J. occidentalis, J. osteosperma
- J. scopulorum, J. virginiana
- J. chinensis, J. virginiana

LARIX
❈ LARCH
●● CLIMATE REGIONS
☼ ◑ SUN, PARTIAL SHADE
↘ SEEDS, SHELTER

Unlike most cone-bearing trees, larches shed their needles in autumn and grow a fresh crop in spring. Small, seed-bearing cones provide fall and winter food; they look like brown rose blossoms, creating a polka-dot effect as they hang from bare

Juniperus with indigo bunting

Larix decidua

Liquidambar styraciflua

Magnolia grandiflora

limbs. These graceful trees reach 30 to 60 feet high in gardens. In eastern regions, a small worm may attack immature foliage, spoiling a tree's appearance for the season.

RECOMMENDED:
- L. decidua, L. kaempferi, L. occidentalis
- L. occidentalis

LIQUIDAMBAR styraciflua
❈ AMERICAN SWEET GUM
●●● CLIMATE REGIONS
☼ SUN
↘ SEEDS, SHELTER

Large, maplelike leaves offer shelter—and a range of fall colors. Bare winter branches reveal seed-bearing fruits: spiky balls hanging on slender stalks. Mature trees reach about 60 feet high and about half that wide. Grove plantings are especially attractive in gardens. In time, surface roots can become intrusive, so plan carefully what you grow nearby.

RECOMMENDED:
- Not grown in desert

MAGNOLIA
❈ ❈ MAGNOLIA
●● CLIMATE REGIONS
☼ ◑ SUN, PARTIAL SHADE
↘ SEEDS, SHELTER

Dense canopies of large leaves shelter birds, and conelike seed vessels provide food. Evergreen species are preferred for their year-round foliage cover. Southern magnolia *(M. grandiflora)* grows to 80 feet, producing fragrant, waxy white flowers against polished, dark green leaves. Sweet bay *(M. virginiana)* features smaller, fragrant blossoms and smaller leaves of soft, grayish green on a large shrub or tree to 60 feet. Both magnolias need regular moisture; sweet bay will grow in nearly swampy soils.

RECOMMENDED:
- M. grandiflora
- M. grandiflora, M. virginiana

MALUS

🌳 CRABAPPLE

● ● ● ● ● CLIMATE REGIONS

☼ SUN

🔽 FRUIT, SHELTER

These 20- to 30-foot trees, kin to apples, have tart fruits with strong bird appeal. Fruits can be as small as cranberries or as large as small apples. Spring flowers cover trees in white, pink, or red. Many species and named hybrids are sold. The following all bear fruit regularly—late into the year for those marked 🍎: 'Adams', *M. atrosanguinea* 🍎, *M. baccata*, 'Blanche Ames', 'Dolgo', 'Dorothea', 'Flame', *M. floribunda*, 'Katherine' 🍎, 'Pink Spires', *M. purpurea* 'Lemoinei', 'Radiant' 🍎, 'Royalty', *M. scheideckeri*, 'Sissipuk' 🍎, 'Snowdrift' 🍎, and 'Vanguard'.

MORUS

🌳 MULBERRY

● ● ● ● ● ● CLIMATE REGIONS

☼ SUN

🔽 FRUIT, SHELTER

Blackberrylike fruits are treats for birds in late spring and early summer. Not all mulberries bear fruit; be sure to choose a species that does. White mulberry (*M. alba*) and red mulberry (*M. rubra*) reach about 50 feet high with broadly rounded foliage canopies. Persian mulberry (*M. nigra*) grows to about 30 feet. Mulberries adapt to a wide range of soils and climates; surface roots compete with other plants grown beneath the foliage. Fallen fruits can stain pavement.

RECOMMENDED:

● ● ● *M. alba*, *M. nigra*

● *M. alba*, *M. rubra*

MYRICA

🌳 WAX MYRTLE

● ● ● CLIMATE REGIONS

☼ SUN

🔽 FRUIT

Pacific wax myrtle (*M. californica*) and southern wax myrtle (*M. cerifera*) form

Malus (crabapple)

Morus with brown thrasher

Myrica cerifera

Picea with gray catbird
Pinus with great horned owl

upright, shrubby trees to about 30 feet—neat but undramatic, with glossy, narrow leaves. Inconspicuous male and female flowers are borne on separate plants; in fall and winter, if there's a male plant nearby, female plants have waxy grayish purple berries that attract birds. For a *Myrica* shrub, see page 63.

RECOMMENDED:

● ● *M. californica*; not grown in desert

● *M. cerifera*

PICEA

🌳 SPRUCE

● ● ● ● CLIMATE REGIONS

☼ SUN

🔽 SEEDS, SHELTER

Needle-leafed branches offer year-round shelter, and seeds carried in hanging cones provide food. Many spruce species are quite tall—rigidly upright, cone-shaped or pyramidal—but nurseries offer shorter selections; needles can be dark green to silvery blue. Most spruces do best in northern latitudes or higher altitudes, where summers are cool or mild, not hot and humid.

RECOMMENDED:

● ● *P. engelmannii*, *P. pungens*

● *P. glauca*, *P. pungens*

● *P. engelmannii*, *P. glauca*

PINUS

🌳 PINE

● ● ● ● ● CLIMATE REGIONS

☼ SUN

🔽 SEEDS, SHELTER

Widely adapted, these cone-bearing, needle-leafed trees provide yearlong bird shelter in all climates. Seeds ("pine nuts") in the cones are sought by many birds. Some pines mature at 30 to 40 feet; others top out at over 100 feet. Growth in some is upright and narrow; in others, rounded or irregular. Needles vary from 2 inches to more than 1 foot long, from stiff to almost limp. Choose a species that offers dense foliage.

PRUNUS

🌳 🌳 CHERRY, PLUM

● ● ● ● ● ● CLIMATE REGIONS

☼ SUN

⤳ FRUIT, SHELTER

Besides cherries edible by humans, many other cherries and plums are good choices strictly for the birds. In spring, white or pink blossoms cover the bare branches of deciduous kinds; fruits follow in summer, and autumn brings yellow, orange, or red leaf color. Evergreen species are gigantic shrubs with purple to blue-black cherries; spring flowers don't qualify as showy. Cherry and plum fruits can be messy if they fall on pavement.

RECOMMENDED:

● ● *P. cerasifera* 'Allred',
P. c. 'Atropurpurea', *P. ilicifolia*,
P. lyonii

● *P. cerasifera* 'Allred',
P. c. 'Atropurpurea', *P. maackii*,
P. padus

● *P. americana*, *P. pensylvanica*,
P. serotina

● *P. caroliniana*, *P. cerasifera* 'Allred',
P. c. 'Atropurpurea', *P. padus*,
P. pensylvanica, *P. serotina*

● *P. cerasifera* 'Allred',
P. c. 'Atropurpurea', *P. padus*,
P. pensylvanica, *P. serotina*

QUERCUS

🌳 🌳 OAK

● ● ● ● ● ● CLIMATE REGIONS

☼ SUN

⤳ ACORNS, INSECTS, SHELTER

All oaks bear acorns—food for many birds—though the size and shape of both nuts and trees vary greatly. Foliage canopies give good nesting sites and also harbor insects for additional bird meals. Species include evergreen oaks for mild climates and deciduous ones for both cold-winter and milder regions.

RECOMMENDED:

● *Q. agrifolia*, *Q. chrysolepis*,
Q. douglasii, *Q. garryana*,
Q. kelloggii

Prunus (plum)

Quercus

Sassafras albidum

Sorbus aucuparia

○ *Q. agrifolia*, *Q. chrysolepis* (not in desert), *Q. douglasii*, *Q. emoryi*, *Q. engelmannii* (not in desert), *Q. wislizenii* (not in desert)

● *Q. bicolor*, *Q. gambelii*,
Q. macrocarpa

● *Q. macrocarpa*, *Q. stellata*

SASSAFRAS albidum

🌳 SASSAFRAS

● ● CLIMATE REGIONS

☼ SUN

⤳ FRUIT, SHELTER

These picturesquely sculptured trees yield black berries that feed several bird species in autumn. Individual trees can be self-fertile, assuring a fruit crop, or may bear only male or female flowers, requiring a separate pollinator tree for a female tree to fruit. Determining which you have at the nursery is difficult. Trees grow quickly to 25 feet and can ultimately reach 60 feet. Fall foliage is orange, red, and copper.

SORBUS

🌳 MOUNTAIN ASH

● ● ● ● ● CLIMATE REGIONS

☼ ◐ SUN, PARTIAL SHADE

⤳ FRUIT, SHELTER

Clusters of small white flowers, showy berries (generally red), and colorful fall foliage offer changing interest. To birds, the fruits are what count. Several species are available, all fairly fast growing, medium to tall. They tolerate heat and cold but dislike the extreme heat of the lower Midwest, Southeast, and Southwest; they need summer moisture.

RECOMMENDED:

● *S. alnifolia*, *S. aucuparia*

● ● *S. alnifolia*, *S. aucuparia*,
S. decora; not grown in hottest regions

● *S. alnifolia*, *S. decora*; not grown in hottest regions

● *S. alnifolia*; not grown in hottest regions

THUJA
✤ ARBORVITAE
◉ ◉ ◌ CLIMATE REGIONS
☀ ● SUN, SUMMER SHADE IN
HOT AREAS
➹ SEEDS, SHELTER

Small cones furnish seeds to feed birds; year-round, scalelike foliage gives shelter. Neat and symmetrical, these trees perform best in regions with moist soil (well-drained) and atmosphere. *T. occidentalis,* a 40- to 60-foot tree, is less widely available than shrubbier forms of the species; severe cold turns foliage brownish. Western red cedar *(T. plicata)* can reach 100 feet or higher, with wide-spreading lower branches.

RECOMMENDED:
◉ *T. plicata*
◉ *T. occidentalis*
◌ *T. occidentalis, T. plicata*

Thuja plicata

Tsuga caroliniana

TSUGA
✤ HEMLOCK
◉ ◉ ◉ ◌ CLIMATE REGIONS
☀ ◐ SUN, PARTIAL SHADE
➹ SEEDS, SHELTER

Horizontal to drooping branches with flat, needlelike leaves create a dense and feathery effect. Small brown cones hang from the branches, providing eagerly consumed seeds. *T. canadensis* and *T. caroliniana* can reach 70 feet, and *T. heterophylla* even taller, but all three can also be maintained as handsome clipped hedges. Hemlocks like atmospheric moisture, summer rain, and regular soil moisture; they need some winter chill. Plant them where they'll be sheltered from strong wind.

RECOMMENDED:
◉ ◉ *T. heterophylla*
◌ *T. canadensis, T. caroliniana*

GRASSES FOR BIRDS—NOT FOR MOWING

Grasses add dramatic contrasts and movement to garden designs. In bird gardens, their fine-textured foliage and delicate seed heads are both ornamental and functional. Birds seek them out in the garden just as they do in the wild for food, shelter, and nesting materials.

You can plant ornamental grasses in sunny beds and borders as accents, or intermingle them with shrubs and perennials. Or consider creating a "grasscape"—a natural landscape that incorporates a variety of ornamental grasses with wildflowers and other plants. These aren't grasses for mowing; instead, they contribute fountains of foliage with minimal care on your part.

Many ornamental grasses will naturalize readily in open meadows, on hillsides, or along roadways; make sure your choices aren't considered invasive in your geographical region.

Along with such familiar landscaping grasses as feather grass *(Stipa)* and fountain grass *(Pennisetum),* you might also want to seek out one or more of the following bird favorites:

Panicum virgatum

BIG BLUESTEM (Andropogon gerardii): Sun-loving prairie grass with arching foliage clumps 4 to 8 feet tall.

INDIAN GRASS (Sorghastrum nutans): Clumping prairie grass with 5- to 7-foot flower stalks; reseeds readily in moist sites.

INDIAN RICE GRASS (Oryzopsis hymenoides): Fine-textured grass with heavy seed crop, dormant by summer but golden into winter; best in arid locations.

LITTLE BLUESTEM (Schizachyrium scoparium): Clumps 2 to 4 feet tall found on eastern dry hills, open woods, prairies; tends to reseed.

PRAIRIE CORD GRASS (Spartina pectinata): Most useful along water in native freshwater marshlands and coastal habitats where its aggressive spreading habits are welcome.

PURPLE-TOP (Tridens flavus): Native eastern field grass, highly adaptable but prefers moist, fertile, open sites.

SWITCH GRASS (Panicum virgatum): One of the most adaptable ornamental grasses, with sturdy 4- to 7-foot-tall clumps that stay upright through winter.

SHRUBS

Shrubs furnish "layering" in a birdscape, forming a bridge between trees and open space. They're valuable both for food and protective cover, including nesting sites—and a grouping that approximates a natural thicket is even

Amelanchier with blue jay

Arctostaphylos densiflora 'Howard McMinn'

Heteromeles arbutifolia

better than a single shrub. Dense shrubbery can make a good hideaway from a feline hunter, and thorny shrubs are an especially effective cover from predators. Evergreen shrubs provide muchneeded winter shelter where temperatures drop low.

Some shrubby plants function as trees in their larger size ranges; these are described beginning on page 50. Shrubs that are favorites of hummingbirds are listed on page 71. For desert shrubs that appeal to birds, see page 53.

Aronia arbutifolia with rose-breasted grosbeak

AMELANCHIER
🌿 SERVICEBERRY, SHADBLOW
- ● ● ● ● ● CLIMATE REGIONS
- ☼ SUN
- ⤳ FRUIT

Dark blue berries feed a great variety of birds in summer, but these graceful, medium-size to large shrubs are attractive in all seasons. White or blush flowers bloom in early spring; emerging foliage is pink, bronze red, or purple, maturing to green; in autumn, leaves change to yellow, orange, or red. (For tree-size species, see page 51.)

RECOMMENDED:
- ● ● ● A. alnifolia
- ● ● A. grandiflora, A. stolonifera

ARCTOSTAPHYLOS
🌿 MANZANITA
- ● ● CLIMATE REGIONS
- ☼ SUN
- ⤳ BLOSSOMS, FRUIT, INSECTS

Attractions for birds include blossoms in late winter and early spring, fruits like pea-size apples in later spring or summer, and insects. Most manzanitas are Pacific Coast natives successful only in that region. Many have smooth-barked branches of dark bronze to wine red; oval leaves of bright green to nearly blue-gray; and small, clustered white or pink flowers. Most need well-drained soil and won't tolerate much summer water. These shrubs can be as large as small trees, but gardeners in Middle Atlantic, northern, and Pacific Coast states use A. uva-ursi—bearberry—as a low ground cover.

RECOMMENDED:
- ● Not in desert

ARONIA
🌿 CHOKEBERRY
- ● ● ● ● CLIMATE REGIONS
- ☼ SUN
- ⤳ FRUIT

Fruits begin to ripen in late summer and last into winter: red (A. arbutifolia), purple (A. prunifolia), or black (A. melanocarpa). Leaves and white or pinkish little flowers precede them in spring. Plants are fairly upright, spreading into clumps. Red and purple chokeberries reach 10 feet; black, only half that.

RECOMMENDED:
- ● A. arbutifolia, A. melanocarpa
- ● A. arbutifolia

BERBERIS
🌿 🌿 BARBERRY
- ● ● ● ● ● CLIMATE REGIONS
- ☼ ◑ SUN, PARTIAL SHADE
- ⤳ FRUIT, SHELTER

Red, blue, or black fruits can be showy, but birds usually turn to them only after other berry sources have been stripped. The dense and usually thorny plants do offer popular shelter and nest sites. Hardiness varies, as do size and shape; all species are noted for toughness in a variety of climates and soils. Most have small but attractive yellow or orange flowers and small leaves; deciduous kinds offer bright autumn color. Barberries make good impenetrable hedges.

CALLICARPA
❁ BEAUTYBERRY

● ● ● ● ● CLIMATE REGIONS
☼ ◑ SUN, LIGHT SHADE
❧ FRUIT

Violet to purple autumn berries are both garden ornaments and bird lures. Spring flowers are inconspicuous on upright or arching 6- to 10-foot plants. Stems may freeze to the ground in severe winters, but this doesn't stop fruit production. Flowers (and then berries) are borne on new wood produced in spring.

RECOMMENDED:
● ● C. americana, C. bodinieri giraldii, C. japonica
○ C. americana, C. bodinieri giraldii, C. japonica; not grown in desert
● ● C. bodinieri giraldii, C. japonica

CORNUS
❁ DOGWOOD

● ● ● ● ● CLIMATE REGIONS
☼ ◑ SUN, PARTIAL SHADE
❧ FRUIT, INSECTS, SHELTER

Shrubby dogwoods don't have flower power equal to the tree dogwoods (page 51), but they appeal to birds with the same berrylike fruits ripening from summer to fall. An insect population adds to the allure. Several species are widely sold, all forming upright clumps to about 10 to 15 feet high; all prefer moist soil. All have an autumn foliage show; some have colored stems.

Those with bright red winter stems include Tatarian dogwood (*C. alba*),

Berberis with Bullock's oriole

Callicarpa americana

Cornus amomum

Cotoneaster lacteus

❁ EVERGREEN ❁ DECIDUOUS
● NORTHERN PACIFIC COAST
● SOUTHERN PACIFIC COAST, LOW DESERT
● MOUNTAINS, GREAT BASIN, HIGH DESERT
● PLAINS AND PRAIRIES
● SOUTHEAST ○ NORTHEAST
❧ VALUE TO BIRDS

bloodtwig dogwood (*C. sanguinea*), and redtwig (or red-osier) dogwood (*C. stolonifera*), which spreads by underground stems into clumps. For coral stems, choose Siberian dogwood (*C. alba* 'Sibirica'), a shorter plant to about 7 feet. *C. stolonifera* 'Flaviramea' is described by its common name, yellowtwig dogwood.

RECOMMENDED:
● ● C. alba, C. sanguinea, C. stolonifera
○ C. alba, C. stolonifera
● C. alba, C. amomum, C. mas, C. racemosa, C. stolonifera
○ C. alba, C. mas, C. racemosa, C. stolonifera

COTONEASTER
❁ ❁ COTONEASTER

● ● ● ● ● CLIMATE REGIONS
☼ SUN
❧ FRUIT, SHELTER

Small, applelike red fruits are a great ornament in fall and winter until birds find them. There are plants for nearly all climates, with varied growth habits: tall and arching (some to 18 feet) or simply bushy, low-spreading or ground-hugging. Most have small white flowers in spring, followed by red, coral, or orange berries in autumn. All are easy-care plants that grow vigorously, even in rather poor soil.

ELAEAGNUS
❁ ❁ SILVERBERRY

● ● ● ● ● CLIMATE REGIONS
☼ SUN
❧ FRUIT, SHELTER

Birds are lured by olivelike berries (red or brownish red), shelter, and nesting sites protected by spiny stems in most species. Inconspicuous but fragrant flowers come in fall on evergreen types; fruit matures in spring. Deciduous species flower in spring; fruits ripen in late summer to autumn. These adaptable shrubs grow rapidly into dense, tough plants, 6 to

15 feet tall, that tolerate heat, wind, indifferent soils. A silver cast suffuses foliage.

RECOMMENDED:
- ● ● ● *E. ebbingei, E. multiflora, E. pungens*
- ● ● *E. commutata, E. multiflora, E. umbellata*
- ● *E. commutata, E. umbellata*

EUONYMUS
🌸 🌸 EUONYMUS
- ● ● ● ● ○ CLIMATE REGIONS
- ☀ ◑ SUN, LIGHT SHADE
- ➷ SEEDS, SHELTER

In autumn, hanging seed capsules—shaped like either miniature hatboxes or strawberries—turn orange, red, or yellow, then split open to expose orange seeds. In deciduous species, this coincides with flamboyant fall foliage. The tallest deciduous kind, *E. europaea*, grows to about 20 feet.

RECOMMENDED:
- ● *E. alata, E. europaea, E. kiautschovica*
- ● *E. alata, E. europaea*
- ● *E. alata, E. americana, E. bungeana semipersistens, E. europaea, E. kiautschovica*
- ● *E. alata, E. americana, E. bungeana semipersistens, E. europaea*

HETEROMELES arbutifolia
🌸 TOYON
- ● ● CLIMATE REGIONS
- ☀ ◑ SUN, PARTIAL SHADE
- ➷ FRUIT, SHELTER

This plant's other name, California holly, provides a clue about its fruits and allure to birds. A dense shrub with glossy, dark green leaves, toyon can be kept at about 10 feet but will become a multitrunked shrub-tree with little encouragement. Large clusters of tiny white flowers in late spring set small berries that ripen to brilliant red in late fall. Although toyon is drought-tolerant, it will accept summer moisture if soil is well-drained.

Elaeagnus pungens

Euonymus alata

Heteromeles arbutifolia

Ilex verticillata with eastern bluebird

Juniperus communis

ILEX
🌸 🌸 HOLLY
- ● ● ● ● CLIMATE REGIONS
- ☀ ◑ SUN, PARTIAL SHADE
- ➷ FRUIT, SHELTER

The most familiar hollies for winter decoration have red berries and spine-edged, shiny green leaves, but there are also hollies with smooth-edged leaves, hollies with variegated foliage, and some that lose their leaves entirely. Berries can be yellow and even black. Nearly all are slow to moderate growers, forming bulky, dense shrubs as low as knee-high or as high as 20 feet. Evergreen kinds afford welcome winter shelter. Most hollies bear inconspicuous male and female flowers on separate plants, requiring a pollinating male plant for berry production on the female plant. (See page 52 for tree-size *Ilex* species.)

RECOMMENDED:
- ○ Not grown in desert
- ● *I. glabra, I. laevigata, I. verticillata*

JUNIPERUS
🌸 JUNIPER
- ● ● ● ● ● ○ CLIMATE REGIONS
- ☀ SUN
- ➷ FRUIT, SHELTER

Nearly all shrubby junipers are low-growing forms of species that grow as trees in the wild (see page 54). Junipers are quite widely adapted, and you'll find something that grows in your region no matter where you live. For the greatest benefit to birds as cover, look for shrubs that are at least waist-high. Some will bear fruit, but some won't; the surest guide is to see berries on a plant when you're buying it.

LIGUSTRUM
🌸 🌸 PRIVET
- ● ● ● ● ● ○ CLIMATE REGIONS
- ☀ ◑ SUN, LIGHT SHADE
- ➷ FRUIT, SHELTER

This classic hedge plant, if not formally sheared, offers good shelter and nesting opportunities. (A closely clipped hedge is too dense for birds to enter.) Unsheared privets can grow to 15 feet, displaying tiny white blossoms in spring that later produce blue-black, berrylike fruits to supplement birds' autumn and winter diets. All species thrive with little care in any type of soil.

RECOMMENDED:
- ● ● ● *L. japonicum, L. ovalifolium, L. vulgare*
- ● *L. amurense, L. vulgare*
- ● *L. amurense, L. obtusifolium*
- ● *L. amurense, L. ibolium, L. obtusifolium*

Ligustrum japonicum 'Texanum'

Lindera benzoin

LINDERA benzoin
❀ SPICEBUSH
   ● ● CLIMATE REGIONS
   ☀ SUN
   ➤ FRUIT, SHELTER

From spring leaf-out to autumn's blaze of golden foliage, these dense, twiggy plants offer good shelter. Tiny, greenish yellow flowers decorate bare branches in spring and mature to bright red, ½-inch berries in early fall. To ensure berries on a female plant, you need a male plant nearby. Plants grow to 15 feet.

LONICERA
❀ ❀ HONEYSUCKLE
   ● ● ● ● ● CLIMATE REGIONS
   ☀ ◑ SUN, PARTIAL SHADE
   ➤ BLOSSOMS, FRUIT, INSECTS, SHELTER

Honeysuckles in shrub form offer a varied bird banquet: fruits, insects, and nectar-bearing flowers for hummingbirds. Fragrant blossoms are white or pink; small red or purple fruits ripen in summer or autumn. Plants are arching or rounded, from 6 to 15 feet high. Two exceptions are evergreen box honeysuckle *(L. nitida)*, an erect 6-footer, and 4-foot semievergreen privet honeysuckle *(L. pileata)*, with horizontal branches. Honeysuckles are vigorous and unfussy,

Lonicera tatarica

Mahonia aquifolium

Malus sargentii

thriving in many climates and soils. (For vining honeysuckles, see page 69.)

RECOMMENDED:
- ● *L. fragrantissima, L. korolkowii, L. tatarica*
- ● *L. fragrantissima, L. korolkowii, L. maackii, L. tatarica*
- ● *L. maackii, L. morrowii, L. tatarica*
- ● *L. bella, L. fragrantissima, L. korolkowii, L. nitida, L. pileata*
- ● *L. bella, L. maackii, L. morrowii, L. tatarica*

MAHONIA
❀ MAHONIA
   ● ● CLIMATE REGIONS
   ☀ ◑ SUN, PARTIAL SHADE
   ➤ FRUIT, SHELTER

Handsome hollylike leaflets offer safe haven to birds in *M. aquifolium* (Oregon grape) and other dense-growing species. Yellow spring flowers at branch tips are followed by summer and early autumn fruits, usually blueberrylike. Like the fruits of closely related *Berberis* (barberry), these are eaten only after more favored fruits are gone. Numerous stems rise from the roots, branching to form a spreading plant. Most mahonias reach about 6 feet high—or can be pruned to stay at that height.

RECOMMENDED:
- ● *M. aquifolium, M. pinnata*
- ● *M. aquifolium, M. fremontii, M. nevinii, M. pinnata* (not grown in desert)

MALUS sargentii
❀ SARGENT CRABAPPLE
   ● ● ● ● CLIMATE REGIONS
   ☀ SUN
   ➤ FRUIT, SHELTER

This shrubby type of crabapple offers plentiful dark red fruits that appear in fall and last (if not eaten) into winter. Dense foliage and zigzag branching offer good sanctuary. A lavish display of small white
Continued on page 63 >

PROTECTING GARDEN CROPS

Gardeners who grow fruits and vegetables are likely to make a frustrating discovery—birds think they've been invited to a neighborhood potluck! Some gardeners plant more than they need and simply plan to sacrifice a portion of it. But if you're counting on harvesting everything you've planted, you'll need to take protective measures.

CROP COVERS. The only surefire way to save a crop is to cover it so that birds can't get to it. The simplest method is to drape plants with flexible nylon or vinyl-coated bird netting, sold in rolls or large pieces; the small mesh (generally ½-inch) keeps birds out. Look for bird netting at agricultural supply, feed and grain, or hardware stores. With careful handling, netting can last several years.

To work, netting must completely cover plants—easiest with cane berries and other short plants, more of a project with a tree. Enclose each tree with netting 2 or 3 weeks before fruit ripens. If feasible, suspend netting a couple of inches from fruit, or else birds will simply perch on it to peck at the fruit. Secure netting to the ground or gather it around the tree trunk. Remove netting right after harvest so branches don't grow through and make it difficult to get off later.

Reaching beneath netting to pick fruit can be a challenge. Though it entails greater effort and cost, you can design a cage for easy access; build frames to fit your plants and cover with bird netting or ½-inch poultry wire.

Row crops such as strawberries and peas can also be protected with plastic netting or ½-inch chicken wire, held up by wooden or plastic pipe frames. To protect newly planted seeds and young seedlings, spread plastic or wire mesh screening or floating row covers over beds for 4 to 6 weeks, until stems are sturdy and leaves are less succulent. To make portable row protectors, cover a frame (hoops or inverted triangles of scrap lumber) with cheesecloth or screening. In warm areas, remove fabric covers as the weather heats up—even porous material will trap heat.

SCARE DEVICES. From inflatable owls to reflective tape—or old-fashioned scarecrows—scare devices are designed to take advantage of birds' natural wariness. The problem is that birds quickly catch on that these devices pose no real harm. For best results, use a variety of tactics and change them every few days.

One popular device is flash tape. Try suspending this reflective tape loosely between stakes 6 to 8 inches above row crops, or stretch and then twist the tape between stakes alongside the rows. As the tape vibrates in the wind, it creates a strobe effect. Flash tape can also be wrapped around fruit trees.

You can try hanging pie tins in tree branches or stretching streamers of tin can tops, foil strips, jar lids, glass pieces, shiny fabric, or even colored feathers. Noisy pinwheels or whirligigs are sometimes effective.

DECOY FRUITS. Some gardeners grow decoy fruits, on the theory that birds will ignore your crop if they have something they like even better. To be effective, the decoy crop must ripen at the same time that yours does, and it must be even more alluring. Generally, birds appreciate a tarter taste in fruits than humans do. Still, if your crops are sweet cane berries and blueberries, you may not be able to lure birds away. But decoy plantings of these berries can divert birds from casually damaging larger fruits, such as apples, pears, and plums.

> **THIRSTY?**
>
> If birds are drilling holes in your ripening tomatoes, they may be doing this because they're thirsty. If you keep a birdbath nearby full of fresh water, they'll be more likely to leave your tomatoes alone.

flowers in spring produces clusters of pea-size fruits that ripen before leaves turn color; 'Rosea' has pink blossoms. Rather slow growth eventually reaches about 10 feet high, with a greater spread.

MYRICA pensylvanica
🌿 BAYBERRY
- CLIMATE REGIONS
- ☀ SUN
- ➜ FRUIT, SHELTER

After glossy, aromatic leaves change color and fall off in autumn, you can clearly see the silvery, waxy berries that entice birds in winter. The compact shrub grows to about 9 feet—even in sandy, acid, nutrient-poor soil. Where winter cold isn't severe, plants lose only part of their leaves. You need both male and female plants to get the bird-alluring fruits.

PHOTINIA
🌿 🌿 PHOTINIA
- CLIMATE REGIONS
- ☀ SUN
- ➜ FRUIT, SHELTER

Like their relatives *Heteromeles* (toyon) and *Cotoneaster*, these plants display red berries (black in *P. glabra* when ripe) that ornament autumn and winter landscapes—and attract birds. The large (to 15 feet), dense shrubs all have colorful new foliage and flattened clusters of white flowers in spring.

RECOMMENDED:
- *P. fraseri, P. glabra, P. villosa*
- *P. fraseri, P. glabra*
- *P. villosa*
- *P. glabra*

PRUNUS
🌿 CHERRY, PLUM
- CLIMATE REGIONS
- ☀ SUN
- ➜ FRUIT, SHELTER

Besides the familiar tree species (see page 56), several strictly shrubby cherry

Myrica pensylvanica

Photinia fraseri

Prunus virginiana demissa

Pyracantha with American robin

Rhamnus californica 'Eve Case'

and plum species exist—many native to North America and popular in regions of their origins, and all furnishing cherry-like fruits eagerly consumed by birds in summer. Among non-native species, good choices are Japanese bush cherry (*P. japonica*), growing 4 to 5 feet high, and Nanking cherry (*P. tomentosa*), which reaches 9 feet. Dwarf red-leaf plum (*P. cistena*) has purple leaves on a 6- to 10-foot plant.

RECOMMENDED:
- *P. cistena*
- *P. americana, P. besseyi, P. cistena, P. tomentosa, P. virginiana demissa*
- *P. besseyi, P. cistena, P. japonica, P. tomentosa*

PYRACANTHA
🌿 FIRETHORN
- CLIMATE REGIONS
- ☀ SUN
- ➜ FRUIT, SHELTER

Abundant autumn fruits are renowned for luring birds. In spring, thorny branches are laden with clusters of white flowers set against small, glossy leaves. By late summer or fall, branches blaze with pea-size orange or red fruit. Species and varieties range from big, sprawling shrubs to low, spreading ground covers. They'll grow in almost any soil.

RECOMMENDED:
- *P. coccinea*

RHAMNUS
🌿 🌿 BUCKTHORN
- CLIMATE REGIONS
- ☀ ◑ SUN, PARTIAL SHADE
- ➜ FRUIT, INSECTS, SHELTER

Birds are attracted to these good-looking, easy-to-grow plants both for the red-to-black fruits that appear in autumn and winter and for the resident insect population. These spreading shrubs vary in height (depending on species) from about 12 to 20 feet or more. All are tolerant of poor soil, heat, and less-than-regular watering—but they'll thrive with better soil and routine watering.

RECOMMENDED:
- ● *R. alaternus, R. californica, R. crocea*
- ● *R. alaternus, R. californica, R. crocea ilicifolia* (not grown in desert), *R. frangula*
- ●● *R. cathartica, R. frangula*
- ● *R. frangula*
- ● *R. alnifolia, R. cathartica, R. frangula*

RIBES
❦ CURRANT, GOOSEBERRY
- ●●●● CLIMATE REGIONS
- ☼ ◑ SUN, PARTIAL SHADE
- ➤ FLOWERS, FRUIT, INSECTS

Summer fruits, generally red or black, are popular with birds, but blossoms also attract hummingbirds and some insectivores. Shrubs with thorns are gooseberries; thornless species are currants. The dense growth (mostly in the 4- to 12-foot range) offers good shelter, especially if armed with thorns. Species native to North America are good choices in their regions. (Some species are an alternate host to white pine blister rust and may be forbidden in certain areas.)

RECOMMENDED:
- ● *R. aureum, R. sanguineum*
- ● *R. aureum, R. sanguineum* (not grown in desert)
- ● *R. aureum, R. odoratum*
- ● *R. odoratum*

ROSA
❦ ROSE
- ●●●●●● CLIMATE REGIONS
- ☼ ◑ SUN, PARTIAL SHADE
- ➤ FRUIT, SHELTER

Birds prefer roses that produce a tangle of thorny stems and bear clusters of small fruits ("rose hips"). Many native North American species fit these specifications, as does the Japanese native *R. multiflora*. Other suitable exotic species

Ribes (currant)

Rosa multiflora with northern cardinals

Rubus (blackberry)

Sambucus canadensis

include the Scotch rose *(R. spinosissima)*, Father Hugo's rose *(R. hugonis)*, sweet brier *(R. eglanteria)*, the Austrian brier *(R. foetida)*, and the species hybrid 'Harison's Yellow'. Some modern hybrid shrub roses also fit the bill.

RUBUS
❦ BRAMBLE
- ●●●●●● CLIMATE REGIONS
- ☼ ◑ SUN, LIGHT SHADE
- ➤ FRUIT, SHELTER

Brambles include all the popular cane berries—blackberry and raspberry, for example—as well as a few strictly ornamental plants. For a bird sanctuary, plant a berry patch and let it grow into a dense, somewhat unruly mound of interlaced canes. Whenever your berry patch gets too untidy, you can cut the canes to the ground and expect the planting to regrow with vigorous new canes.

A good-looking ornamental plant—with fruits edible only by birds—is Rocky Mountain thimbleberry *(R. deliciosus)*. Arching thornless branches to 5 feet high bear showy, single white spring flowers followed by summer fruits.

SAMBUCUS
❦ ELDERBERRY
- ●●●● CLIMATE REGIONS
- ☼ ◑ SUN, LIGHT SHADE
- ➤ FRUIT, SHELTER

Fast-growing elderberries reliably produce heavy crops of berries loved by birds. All species grow into bulky shrubs that can be severely pruned or cut to the ground whenever they become untidy. Large, flattish clusters of tiny white flowers form small red or blue-to-black berries that ripen in summer. Plants thrive in continually moist soil but also tolerate considerable drought.

RECOMMENDED:
- ●●● *S. canadensis, S. pubens, S. racemosa*
- ● *S. canadensis, S. pubens*

SHEPHERDIA
❀ BUFFALOBERRY
● ● ● CLIMATE REGIONS
☀ SUN
↘ FRUIT, SHELTER

Clusters of small red berries in summer are especially appreciated by birds in plains, mountain, and northern regions. Two North American species are cast-iron plants that thrive where frigid winters, hot summers, wind, and poor soil limit landscape choices: *S. argentea* (silver buffaloberry) and *S. canadensis* (russet buffaloberry). Inconspicuous male and female flowers are borne on separate plants; for fruit on the female plant, you need a male plant to pollinate it.

SYMPHORICARPOS
❀ SNOWBERRY, CORALBERRY
● ● ● ● ● CLIMATE REGIONS
☀ ◐ SUN, PARTIAL SHADE
↘ FRUIT, FLOWERS

Showy fruits are useful to a bird's winter diet, but they're consumed only when tastier fare is exhausted. Several species are available, all wispy plants that spread by suckers to form attractive thickets. Small spring flowers may attract hummingbirds; later these form large berries (white or purplish red) on arching stems. Plants do fine with either plentiful or little water.

RECOMMENDED:
● ● ● ● *S. albus, S. chenaultii,*
  S. orbiculatus
● *S. albus, S. orbiculatus*

VACCINIUM
❀ ❀ BLUEBERRY, HUCKLEBERRY
● ● ● CLIMATE REGIONS
☀ ● EXPOSURE NEEDS VARY
↘ FRUIT, SHELTER

Birds are as fond of blueberries and huckleberries as humans are. North America boasts numerous species, varying in size and growth habit; all need acid soil and regular moisture. *V. corymbo-*

Shepherdia argentea

Symphoricarpos albus

Vaccinium (blueberry)

Viburnum trilobum

SAVE IT FOR LATER

Plants that offer "second choice" berries—passed over on the initial go-round because favorite fruits are gobbled up first—can be a good way to extend the banquet season for birds. After the most delectable fruits have been depleted, berries that were initially ignored will provide sustenance as leaner times set in.

---

sum (highbush blueberry), the chief market source, is particularly adapted to the Northeast and Northwest. In the Southeast, similar *V. ashei* (rabbiteye blueberry) is better adapted; grow at least two varieties to set fruit. In western North America, *V. parvifolium* (deciduous red huckleberry) produces red summer fruits on a spreading or cascading plant. Another westerner, *V. ovatum* (evergreen huckleberry), is prized for lustrous foliage—bronze new growth, maturing to dark green.

RECOMMENDED:
● *V. corymbosum, V. ovatum,*
  V. parvifolium
● *V. ashei, V. stamineum*
● *V. corymbosum, V. pallidum*

VIBURNUM
❀ ❀ VIBURNUM
● ● ● ● ● ● CLIMATE REGIONS
☀ ◐ SUN, PARTIAL SHADE
↘ FRUIT, INSECTS, SHELTER

A vast assortment of species and hybrids is as valuable to birds as it is to gardeners. Most bear showy clusters of berrylike fruits (red, blue, or black) that feed birds in autumn and winter. Evergreen *V. tinus* flowers in winter, bearing blue fruits in summer. (Insects in spring and summer supplement the diet.)

Viburnum plicatum tomentosum 'Mariesii'

Most viburnums have handsome, dense foliage that makes good shelter. Deciduous kinds often give a brilliant fall foliage display of yellow, rusty gold, red, or purple. Spring flower clusters, white or pink, later bear fruit—except "snowball" types, which have sterile flowers. Plants range from several feet high to shrub-tree size. Most aren't particular about soil but do need regular moisture.

A FLOWER GARDEN FOR BIRDS

Although trees, shrubs, and vines create the framework of a bird habitat, many annual and perennial flowers also offer food for birds—and add glorious color to your garden.

A feast for the eyes as well as for the birds, this vibrant flower patch includes zinnias, delphiniums, globe amaranths, salvias, snapdragons, and marigolds.

Some favorite garden annuals and perennials yield eagerly consumed seeds. For a more naturalistic garden scheme, you can sow mixtures of wildflowers that will produce seeds at the end of their blooming season. Just be sure to let flowers remain on plants to develop seed heads. You don't need to feel guilty about not removing spent blossoms or tidying up your garden at the end of the season; you're doing the birds a favor by letting the flower stalks stand.

Many plants also harbor insects, thus providing protein snacks for birds. Some flowers have petals that birds may eat, and some flowering plants even contribute materials for nest-building.

Certain kinds of flowers are powerful attractants for hummingbirds because of the nectar they produce. In the lists on the facing page, these are marked with an asterisk (*). See page 71 for additional nectar-producing plants.

Strive for a combination of annuals and perennials that will add up to a lengthy period of bird appeal. *Annuals* are plants that complete their life cycle in a year or less; many provide a long season of bloom within that time span. *Perennials* live on from year to year, but they usually flower for just one bloom season each year.

When you choose your flowering plants, concentrate on species with abundant seeds, such as those listed opposite. Keep in mind that the greater the variety of plant material you offer, the more different kinds of birds you're likely to interest. For ornamental grasses that provide a welcome seed crop, see page 57.

Goldfinch alights on goldenrod.

Eastern bluebird nibbles on columbine.

ANNUALS

Ageratum (floss flower)
Amaranthus (amaranth)
Antirrhinum majus (snapdragon)*
Calendula
Callistephus chinensis (China aster)
Centaurea cyanus
    (bachelor's button)
Chrysanthemum
Coreopsis
Cosmos
Helianthus annuus (sunflower)
Limonium (statice, sea lavender)
Lobularia maritima (sweet alyssum)
Myosotis (forget-me-not)
Nigella damascena (love-in-a-mist)
Portulaca
Tagetes (marigold)
Tithonia rotundifolia
    (Mexican sunflower)
Tropaeolum (nasturtium)*
*Zinnia**

PERENNIALS

Achillea (yarrow)
Aquilegia (columbine)*
Aster
Campanula (bellflower)
Chrysanthemum
Coreopsis
*Delphinium**
Digitalis (foxglove)*
Echinacea purpurea
    (purple coneflower)
Eschscholzia (California poppy)
Eupatorium (Joe Pye weed)
Gaillardia (blanket flower)
Helianthus (sunflower)
Rudbeckia hirta
    (gloriosa daisy, black-eyed Susan)
Scabiosa (pincushion flower)
Solidago (goldenrod)

These plants are hummingbird
favorites.

GROWING YOUR OWN BIRDSEED

Sunflowers are such a favorite food source—so bountiful in seeds and so easy to grow—that you might want to plant a patch of them especially to harvest at season's end. Then you'll have seed to offer in feeders come winter.

Sow seeds of annual sunflowers in the spring where you want the plants to grow in your garden; large-flowered kinds need rich soil.

People prefer to eat the seeds roasted, but birds like them raw. If you don't harvest them, flower heads that are left intact will be a big attraction from fall on into winter.

DON'T PULL THOSE WEEDS!

Do you have an out-of-the-way patch of lawn where you can let the weeds grow at will? Allowing annual wild grasses and grains to grow and go to seed is one way to attract birds. The same is true for perennial weeds; some that birds especially appreciate for their seeds include dandelion, dock, fennel, plantain, and thistle. Just make sure the weed seeds aren't growing where they're likely to spread to other parts of your garden.

Plantain

VINES

The tangled growth of climbing vines adds texture and diversity to your landscape, providing safe hideaways and nesting sites for birds and offering them a menu of nectar, fruits, seeds, and insects. Vines are basically flexible shrubs that just keep on growing. Some attach themselves to surfaces by means of suctioned discs or clinging rootlets; others wrap twining stems or tendrils around supports. Some vines simply clamber upward by threading their way through and over other plants. Most vines benefit from some training and support to get them going in the right direction, but birds will be happiest if you don't get carried away with your pruning.

Vine choices especially attractive to hummingbirds are listed on page 71.

Lonicera japonica

AMPELOPSIS brevipedunculata
❦ BLUEBERRY CLIMBER, PORCELAIN BERRY

●●○●●○ CLIMATE REGIONS

☼ ● SUN OR SHADE

↘ FRUIT, SHELTER

Clusters of grapelike berries attract birds in late summer and early fall. Berries are greenish ivory when immature, then ripen to a striking metallic blue. This vine is a rampant climber to 20 feet, needing sturdy support. The large leaves color up and drop off in fall, but in mild climates new leaves emerge in winter. Full sun produces the most fruit.

Ampelopsis brevipedunculata

BERCHEMIA scandens
❦ SUPPLEJACK

● CLIMATE REGIONS

☼ ◐ SUN, PARTIAL SHADE

↘ FRUIT

Birds in the Southeast frequent this native twining vine for its summer-to-autumn clusters of small, blue-black fruits. Handsome oblong leaves have distinctive parallel veins. A woodland native, supplejack reaches 15 to 20 feet and will scramble over fences or garden shrubs for a naturalistic effect.

Berchemia scandens

CELASTRUS scandens
❦ AMERICAN BITTERSWEET

●●●● CLIMATE REGIONS

☼ SUN

↘ SEEDS, SHELTER

In autumn, conspicuous yellow to orange seed capsules split open to reveal bright red seeds. Plants are male or female; you need a nearby male vine to get fruits on the female. Large, light green oval leaves turn bright yellow in fall. Impressively vigorous, twining branches reach 20 feet or more and may need restraint to keep them from overwhelming neighboring plants. This is a good choice for outlying garden areas or poor soil; in more favorable conditions, this vine can be too successful.

Celastrus scandens with mockingbird

Cocculus carolinus

COCCULUS carolinus
❦ ❦ CAROLINA MOONSEED

● CLIMATE REGIONS

☼ ◐ SUN, PARTIAL SHADE

↘ FRUIT

Showy small red fruits offer summer food to birds in this vine's native Southeast, where it scrambles through shrubs and trees. Restrained growth twines to 12 feet, densely covered with glossy 4-inch

leaves. Male and female flowers are on the same plant, ensuring fruit. Deciduous in colder areas, the vine is evergreen or nearly so in coastal regions and in the lower South.

EUONYMUS fortunei 'Vegetus'

❀ BIG-LEAF WINTER CREEPER

● ● ● ● ○ CLIMATE REGIONS

☼ ● SUN OR SHADE

➴ SEEDS, SHELTER

Of all the vining, ground-cover, and dual-purpose varieties encompassed by *Euonymus fortunei*, this one is the best for birds. Big-leaf winter creeper offers an autumn crop of red seeds in orange capsules—also dense shelter amid its dark green leaves. It will grow as a mounding shrub or attach itself to support (with assistance) as a shrubby vine.

LONICERA

❀ ❀ HONEYSUCKLE

● ● ● ● ● ○ CLIMATE REGIONS

☼ ◐ SUN, PARTIAL SHADE

➴ FLOWERS, FRUIT, INSECTS, SHELTER

Once established, these dense, twining vines provide good shelter. Fragrant tubular flowers entice hummingbirds; pea-size red or black berries may follow in late summer and early autumn.

Among numerous species and varieties, the vigorous evergreen Hall's honeysuckle (*L. japonica* 'Halliana') builds a tangled thatch of stems and bears white blossoms aging to yellow. Red berries and yellow-orange to red blossoms distinguish trumpet honeysuckle (*L. sempervirens*). Woodbine (*L. periclymenum*) bears fragrant creamy flowers, then red berries, especially profuse in yellow-flowered 'Berries Jubilee'; plants are evergreen where winter is mild, deciduous in colder regions.

Honeysuckles are not particular about soil but do require some training. For shrubby honeysuckles, see page 61.

Euonymus fortunei 'Vegetus'

Lonicera sempervirens

Parthenocissus quinquefolia

Vitus (wild) with Carolina chickadee

PARTHENOCISSUS

❀ BOSTON IVY, VIRGINIA CREEPER

● ● ● ● ● ○ CLIMATE REGIONS

☼ ● SUN OR SHADE

➴ FRUIT, SHELTER

For birds, these vines hold the promise of a crop of small, dark, grapelike fruits in autumn. *P. tricuspidata* (Boston ivy) gives dense cover; *P. quinquefolia* (Virginia creeper) has looser, more open growth. The brilliant autumn foliage of both species is legendary, and both are immensely vigorous when established.

Parthenocissus tricuspidata

VITIS

❀ GRAPE

● ● ● ● ● ● CLIMATE REGIONS

☼ ◐ SUN, PARTIAL SHADE

➴ FRUIT, SHELTER

As popular with birds as with humans, grapes provide an abundance of clustered fruit and—when thick vines are trained over arbors—shelter and nesting sites. If a vine is allowed to scramble over other shrubs, it will form a tentlike bird refuge (at the expense of the host shrubs). Nearly all parts of North America have native or adapted grapevines that benefit birds. Not all grapes will grow everywhere, but there's a grape for every part of the country. All are far-reaching (if not pruned), climbing by means of twining tendrils, and most have showy fall foliage color.

❀ EVERGREEN ❀ DECIDUOUS

● NORTHERN PACIFIC COAST

○ SOUTHERN PACIFIC COAST, LOW DESERT

● MOUNTAINS, GREAT BASIN, HIGH DESERT

● PLAINS AND PRAIRIES

● SOUTHEAST ○ NORTHEAST

➴ VALUE TO BIRDS

ACROBATS IN THE GARDEN— HUMMINGBIRDS

Darting from flower to flower, its wings a blur of speed, the tiny hummingbird outmaneuvers anything else in the sky as it gathers nectar and tiny insects. It can rocket straight up, swoop straight down, fly backward or upside down, and hover with ease, picking off insects in midflight.

The hummingbird's rapid wing beats and almost ceaseless animation require extraordinary energy: It must constantly refuel. In a day, one bird can consume more than half its weight in sugar.

Because hummingbirds must feed from dawn to dusk, a yard full of their favorite flowers will attract their attention. Depending on where you live, you might see any of 18 species of hummingbirds that head out of Mexico in late winter for flower-rich breeding grounds to the north. A few migrate as far north as Canada—and some rufous hummingbirds fly all the way to southeast Alaska.

The farther south you are, the more species you are likely to see. In general, hummingbirds migrate north through the lowlands and south (from July on) through both lowlands and mountainous regions, where wildflowers bloom latest.

Only the Costa's and Anna's hummingbirds winter north of Mexico, in mild-weather regions of the West. Some 300 other hummingbird species don't cross the border at all but remain in the sun belt from Mexico southward to Argentina.

HOSTING HUMMERS

Plan your hummingbird garden so that it offers blossoms and perches at different levels (but not much lower than 18 inches)—trees flanked by shrubs, bordered by perennials and annuals. Even on a small patio, you can place a favored vine against a fence, then plant annuals and perennials at its base and in containers. And hang up a sugar-water feeder or two (hummers are territorial, so you attract more of them by offering multiple feeders); see page 27 for instructions.

Hummingbirds visit a huge array of plants—with flowers in all shapes, sizes, colors, and degrees of fragrance—but they do favor some. Classic hummingbird flowers have mostly red, odorless, trumpet-shaped blossoms that limit competition from insects. (Bees, for example, use fragrance to find flowers, don't see red, and aren't svelte enough to enter narrow flower tubes.) The blossom shape promotes pollination: As the hummingbird probes for nectar with its bill and tongue, pollen to fertilize other plants is deposited on its head and bill.

Plant to give a long succession of blooms. Bright red and orange flowers are preferred, but blue and pink are also popular. All the plants listed on the facing page are favorites of some hummingbird species.

TOP LEFT: Broad-tailed hummingbird male

CENTER: Hummingbird pot brims with nectar-rich perennials. Clockwise from bottom left: red 'Firebird' penstemon, three salvia species in red and purple, and scarlet cape fuchsia *(Phygelius capensis)*. Design: Jean Manocchio.

*Albizia
julibrissin*

VINES

Campsis radicans (trumpet creeper)
Distictis buccinatoria
   (blood-red trumpet vine)
Lonicera (honeysuckle)
Pyrostegia venusta (flame vine)
Phaseolus coccineus
   (scarlet runner bean)
Tecomaria capensis (cape honeysuckle)

Campsis radicans

TREES

Acacia
Albizia julibrissin (silk tree)
Chilopsis linearis (desert willow)
Citrus
Erythrina (coral tree)
Eucalyptus
Liriodendron tulipifera (tulip tree)
Malus (crabapple)
Melia azedarach (chinaberry)

SHRUBS

Abelia
Abutilon (flowering maple)
Buddleia (butterfly bush)
Callistemon (bottlebrush)
Cestrum (night jessamine)
Chaenomeles (flowering quince)
Correa (Australian fuchsia)
Erica (heath)
Feijoa sellowiana (pineapple guava)
Fuchsia
Grevillea
Hibiscus syriacus (rose of Sharon)
Justicia (shrimp plant,
    Brazilian plume flower)
Kolkwitzia (beauty bush)
Lonicera (honeysuckle)
Melaleuca
Ribes (flowering currant)
Rosmarinus officinalis (rosemary)
Weigela

Lupine attracts this broad-tailed
hummingbird female.

Nicotiana

ANNUALS

Antirrhinum majus (snapdragon)
Dianthus barbatu (sweet William)
Impatiens
Nicotiana (flowering tobacco)
Petunia
Phlox drummondii (annual phlox)
Salvia (sage)
Tropaeolum majus (nasturtium)
Zinnia

Chaenomeles

PERENNIALS

Agastache cana (double bubble mint)
Agave
Alcea rosea (hollyhock)
Aloe
Alstroemeria
Anigozanthos flavidus (kangaroo paw)
Aquilegia (columbine)
Asclepias tuberosa (butterfly weed)
Cuphea ignea (cigar plant)
Delphinium
Digitalis (foxglove)
Echium fastuosum (pride of Madeira)
Gladiolus
Heuchera (coral bells)
Impatiens
Ipomopsis aggregata
Ipomopsis rubra
Kniphofia (red-hot poker)
Leonotis leonurus (lion's tail)
Lobelia cardinalis (cardinal flower)
Lobelia laxiflora
Lotus berthelotii (parrot's beak)
Lupinus (lupine)
Lychnis chalcedonica (Maltese cross)
Lychnis coronaria (crown pink)
Mimulus (monkey flower)
Mirabilis jalapa (four o'clock)
Monarda (bee balm)
Pelargonium (geranium)
Penstemon (beard tongue)
Phlox
Phygelius capensis (cape fuchsia)
Salvia (sage)
Zauschneria (California fuchsia)

The birds who come to visit your yard—as they fly, eat, bathe, fight, court, build nests, and raise young—provide an ongoing show that's as ordinary as clouds in the sky and as incredible as a hummingbird's migratory marathon. Soaring up above a roadway, roosting on a roof, or crooning in a treetop, theirs is a drama of life's most basic elements: courting, raising young, looking for food, seeking shelter. Whether they show up singly, in pairs, or in flocks, birds help us to feel more in touch with the natural world.

BACKYARD
BIRDING

To become better acquainted with the birds in your yard, you'll want to learn some of the basic strategies of birding, from observing the markings on a bird to studying its behavior to keeping a record of what you see. You'll want to know what kinds of birds are most likely to visit residential neighborhoods and how to identify them. The more you learn about the birds you see—from their varied plumage to their elaborate nesting rituals—the more you'll enjoy your backyard birdscape.

If you're lucky, backyard bird-watching can provide you with such springtime scenes as a prairie warbler tending to its nest.

A DIVERSE FAMILY TREE

Birds inhabit virtually every niche on the globe's surface capable of supporting life at all. Some 9,700 bird species live in diverse areas from the Arctic to the Antarctic, from rain forests to deserts, from mountains to open seas.

Understanding the biological classification of birds—taxonomy—is the first step toward identifying the species you see in your own backyard.

DNA AND BIRD SPECIES

With the advent of DNA and protein analysis, ornithologists now have at their disposal a precise method of determining the relationships among birds. As a result, bird classification is in flux. Greater understanding of relationships between birds may lead to the division of some traditionally recognized species and the grouping together of others.

UNDERSTANDING TAXONOMY

All birds are grouped in the class *Aves*—just as mammals, reptiles, and so on make up separate classes of animals. The *Aves* category encompasses about 200 bird families around the world. Within these, more than 900 individual species of birds representing about 80 families have been observed on this continent north of Mexico. Approximately one-fifth of these originated in Europe, Asia, the Caribbean, or Mexico and are considered "vagrants"; the rest are indigenous to the continent.

Traditional ornithological classification involves a hierarchy of groupings, each with a Latin name. The Latin designations, following a system established in the 18th century, give each bird an identity that stays the same throughout the world, regardless of the different common names by which it may be known in different countries.

FAMILY REUNION
Five blackbird cousins show family resemblance in wing and tail shape and sharply pointed bills.

Brown-headed cowbird

Bobolink

Western meadowlark

Red-winged blackbird

Baltimore oriole

The mourning dove belongs to the biological order of birds called *Columbiformes.* Scientists consider this order to have evolved earlier than the songbirds that dominate the backyard bird scene.

A red-breasted nuthatch pauses on the knob of a maple tree as it heads down the trunk in search of food. The nuthatch is among numerous species classified as members of the *Passeriformes* order—the world's most highly evolved birds.

The broadest subclassification of the class *Aves* is *order*, followed by *family*; an order can include one or many families of genetically related birds. The order *Passeriformes*, for example, includes dozens of families—three dozen of which are found in North America.

Each family is broken down into still more specialized groupings, starting with *genus*; the genus name always appears, capitalized, as the first word in a bird's scientific name. *Species* is a descriptive term that follows, narrowing the classification further. Bird families may be large, containing a number of related species; or they may be made up of a single species. The *Icteridae* family, for example, represents two dozen blackbird cousins in North America, while the wrentit is the only member of the *Timaliidae* family on this continent.

Some families are also divided into subfamilies, and some species are broken into subspecies. As regional characteristics become clearly defined, from time to time certain subspecies may be reclassified as full species.

Here's how the black-headed grosbeak, *Pheucticus melanocephalus,* is classified:

- ❧ Order—*Passeriformes,* meaning "perching bird."
- ❧ Family—*Cardinalidae,* meaning both "important" and "wearing red."
- ❧ Genus—*Pheucticus,* meaning "painted with cosmetics."
- ❧ Species—*melanocephalus,* meaning "black-headed."

The sequence of classification also reflects the relative level of evolution, as well as relationships between birds. Loons, grebes, and pelicans, for example, are some of North America's most primitive birds—that is, they were among the earliest to evolve. As such, they appear first in most field guides. The most "highly evolved" birds—the ones that came on the scene most recently—are members of the order *Passeriformes;* you'll usually find them listed last in field guides.

BACKYARD BIRD FAMILIES

The bird families most likely to appear in North American residential gardens are represented in the "Garden Guest List" beginning on page 85. They are members of the following taxonomic orders:

Falconiformes—includes falcons

Galliformes—includes pheasants, quail, and several other game birds

Charadriiformes—includes birds such as killdeer that live near water

Columbiformes—includes pigeons and doves

Strigiformes—includes owls

Apodiformes—includes swifts and hummingbirds

Piciformes—includes woodpeckers

Passeriformes (songbirds)—includes many families and nearly two-thirds of the bird species in the world, among them flycatchers, vireos, jays, swallows, chickadees, nuthatches, creepers, wrens, kinglets, thrushes, mockingbirds, starlings, waxwings, warblers, tanagers, sparrows, cardinals, blackbirds, and finches.

The American kestrel has a strong, hooked bill for tearing flesh and crushing bones of prey.

The hairy woodpecker's straight, sturdy bill functions as a chisel to hammer into trees and capture insects.

The ruby-throated hummingbird uses its long, slim bill to extract nectar and insects from flowers.

The red-eyed vireo's bill is a tool for capturing, holding, and crushing insects.

The song sparrow has a heavy, triangular bill to grasp seeds and crush them.

ANATOMY THROUGH EVOLUTION

Over millions of years, birds have adapted to diverse conditions around the globe. For the ostrich and other large, flightless birds inhabiting flat regions, running was the most significant survival skill—thus strong legs became important. The tiny songbird, in contrast, needed to be able to rest after long flights; it developed three toes pointing forward and one pointing backward, thereby enabling it to perch safely.

The ostrich represents a primitive level of bird evolution, while songbirds are considered by ornithologists to be the most anatomically advanced. More than half of the species of birds in the world today belong to the scientific order classified as songbirds—*Passeriformes.*

The earliest birds resembled feathered dinosaurs. Dating from about 150 million years ago, fossils of the *archyaeopteryx* —"ancient wing"— reveal creatures with clawed wings, toothed bills, bony tails, and heavy skeletal structures. It seems unlikely that they did much flying; they probably hopped along the ground or glided from tree to tree.

Birds that looked more like modern forms—such as loons and pelicans—didn't appear until 60 million years ago. One million years ago, the ancestors of today's bird families had come into existence.

SURVIVAL STRATEGIES

Today all birds share certain anatomical characteristics:

- All are warm-blooded, feathered creatures with wings (although not all can fly).

- All have hornlike bills and scaled legs and feet.

- Lightweight, hollow bones enable them to stay airborne, and a clavicle—or wishbone—anchors their massive breast muscles for flight.

However, birds have had to develop many specialized anatomical characteristics in order to survive for so long in the earth's great environmental diversity. In the process, they have evolved into organisms

This female northern cardinal perches with ease, thanks to her arrangement of toes—three forward, one backward.

A shock-absorbing body structure permits the red-bellied woodpecker to pound away at tree trunks with its bill.

as marvelously varied as the geographical areas they frequent.

BILLS. Every size and shape have evolved to assure successful feeding in diverse habitats. Most ducks, for example, have broad, spatulate bills that can sift aquatic plant and animal food from muddy water. Pelicans have enough room in their bills to carry a hearty portion of fish.

Woodpeckers have specialized bills, bones, and muscles to absorb the impact of hammering into trees as they search for wood-boring insects. They have also evolved an extremely long tongue for capturing insects deep inside drilled holes or crevices.

The broad bills of seedeaters such as grosbeaks, finches, and sparrows are specially designed to crack seed hulls open. By contrast, such birds as vireos, wrens, warblers, and flycatchers have thinner bills for snatching insects.

FEET AND WINGS. A duck's webbed feet are adapted for swimming; a woodpecker's large feet and broad tail keep the bird stable while it clings to trees to drill for food. The feet of ground-feeding birds, such as the brown thrasher, are often proportionately larger than those of birds that glean insects from leafy vegetation, such as chickadees or warblers.

The long, pointed wings of falcons and swallows have evolved for swift flying over long distances. The comparatively short wings of wrens, on the other hand, are adapted for quick shuttles from one clump of shrubbery to another. An owl's specialized feather structure allows it to fly silently through the night in search of small prey, such as deer mice, that would be alerted by a noisier approach.

Barn swallow

Birds have evolved a variety of flight techniques, too. Small songbirds flap their wings in energetic up-and-down strokes. Tiny hummingbirds hover as they beat their wings 70 times per second. Hawks soar gracefully on air currents, and most species glide at least occasionally. Bigger birds glide more slowly and over longer distances.

The penguin uses its wings as flippers after diving into icy arctic water; its swimming motion is the same as the flying movements of other birds. Even though this big bird does not fly, scientists believe that its ancestors once did.

TOES AND TALONS

Owls' talons can capture and kill prey, then hold it while it is eaten.

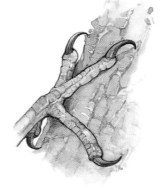

Two forward and two backward toes—along with sharp claws—let woodpeckers cling to vertical tree surfaces.

Quail use sturdy forward toes to scratch the ground for food.

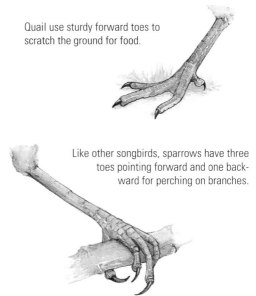

Like other songbirds, sparrows have three toes pointing forward and one backward for perching on branches.

The Baltimore oriole, shown at nest, right, can be distinguished from the similar Bullock's oriole by its all-black hood. The female eastern bluebird, below at birdhouse entrance, is a paler version of the vividly hued male.

A roosting eastern screech-owl almost disappears against tree bark, camouflaged by its coloration.

LEARNING TO TELL WHO'S WHO

Learning to identify birds accurately is basic to birding, at home or afield. Like pieces of a puzzle, your observations about a bird's appearance and behavior can be fitted together to help you put names to the species you see in your yard. Along with the experience you accumulate, the basic tools that will help you to accomplish this are a field guide, a notebook for recording what you observe, and a pair of binoculars (see page 80).

LOOKING FOR CLUES

Birders identify species by exact characteristics, such as wing markings, and also relative ones, such as size. The drawing on the facing page shows the many clues to a bird's identity that its tiny body displays.

COLORS. Often the most obvious field mark is a bird's color: on its back, underside, tail, head, breast, and elsewhere. The hues of some species—such as the painted bunting—are vibrantly obvious, but more subtle tones are characteristic of many birds, such as the eastern phoebe and the pine siskin. And some birds' coloration is designed to keep you from being able to see the bird at all—that is, color and markings make the birds blend perfectly with their surroundings to protect them from predators. Ground-feeding birds are protected by feathers that seem to fade into the surrounding landscape. Other birds "disappear" against the foliage or bark of trees.

Color can tell you whether a bird is a juvenile or an adult, a male or a female. The male of a species is often brightly colored and the female relatively dull—a difference that can serve more than one purpose. The red-winged blackbird, for instance, displays its red epaulettes both to attract a female and to ward off other males competing for its nesting territory.

Birds of the same species may also show color variations in different parts of the country and at different times of the year. Some male birds revert to less gaudy coloration outside their breeding season.

SIZE AND SHAPE. The easiest way to measure a bird's size is to compare it with a familiar bird, such as a sparrow, robin, or crow. Just note whether the bird you are trying to identify is about the same size, smaller, or larger than the known species.

Observing the shape of the bill, head, legs, wings, and tail will help you to differentiate similar species. For example, downy and hairy woodpeckers look almost the same, but the hairy's bill is heavy and about as long as its head—the downy's is thinner and only about half that size.

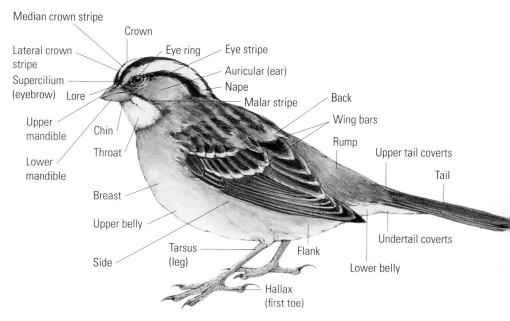

PROFILE OF A WHITE-THROATED SPARROW

Median crown stripe · Crown · Eye ring · Eye stripe · Lateral crown stripe · Auricular (ear) · Supercilium (eyebrow) · Lore · Nape · Back · Malar stripe · Wing bars · Upper mandible · Chin · Rump · Upper tail coverts · Lower mandible · Throat · Tail · Breast · Upper belly · Undertail coverts · Tarsus (leg) · Flank · Lower belly · Side · Hallax (first toe)

MARKINGS. Wing bars, eye rings or stripes, any pattern on the head or neck, or streaking on the back or breast can help you to identify a species. Sometimes a marking such as a spot of color on a bird's crown can distinguish male from female, as with the ruby-crowned kinglet (the female lacks the ruby crown). Sometimes a slight variation in markings is the only way to tell one species from another.

USING A FIELD GUIDE

Your most essential identification tool is a good field guide to the birds in your region. Field guides illustrate and describe birds in a particular geographic area—such as North America or the western United States. Traditionally, guides are organized in taxonomic categories—grouped according to scientific family classifications.

The "Garden Guest List" on pages 85–125 of this book is a good starting place, but your particular area will attract many more species than can be described here. Look for a field guide that's comprehensive for your region, with clear illustrations of each species, range maps, and descriptions that are easy to understand. Don't discount personal preference—you want a guide that suits you and the way you intend to use it.

Study and check off birds in your field guide (or this book) or on a separate checklist as you identify them. If you think you're seeing mostly sparrows and finches, for example, mark these pages with paper clips or paper tabs for easy reference when you want to be able to identify a bird quickly. Use range maps to eliminate species that don't occur in your area.

Even when you see a known bird, such as a robin, look it up to learn more about both the familiar species and other birds that could be mistaken for it. Also read your field guide to learn the migratory patterns of birds that appear only briefly and seasonally in your garden.

KEEPING A RECORD

A birding journal can add richly to the satisfaction you receive from your garden visitors. Such a notebook usually starts as a simple list of the birds seen on a given day. If you can't identify a bird but can narrow down the possibilities to two or three similar species, note their names and anything you noticed that can help you make a more precise identification the next time you see the bird.

Include the date of each observation, the time of day, and the weather conditions. Within a few years, your notebook will start to reflect both seasonal changes and population fluctuations.

As part of your record-keeping, you may want to start a checklist of all the different bird species you see and identify, including the date and place you saw each bird.

CLOSE-UP VIEW: CHOOSING BINOCULARS

Since birding is visual—and because birds are small and quick to fly away—binoculars are important if you want to be able to identify that American tree sparrow or yellow-rumped warbler in your backyard. Here's what you need to consider to choose the right pair for you.

LENSES. Binoculars are commonly sold by a numerical description—7× 35, for example. The first number tells how many times the binoculars magnify the image; the second gives the diameter in millimeters of the objective lenses (the ones farthest from the eyes).

Look for magnification in the 7× to 10× range (go to the higher power if you can hold the binoculars steady, a skill that improves with practice). Greater magnification results in a narrowed field of vision, so if you go too high you won't have a wide enough viewing area to find and follow fast-moving birds.

The wider the objective lenses, the more light they gather and the better you can see in shadow, at dawn, or at dusk—but the heavier the binoculars will be. Opt for large lenses if you'll be using them at twilight or after dark.

As a rule of thumb, divide the second number by the first one (for example, 35 ÷ 7). A dividend of 5 or greater means that the binoculars will provide enough light for birding.

Crowded back to back, hummingbird nestlings come into close view with the aid of binoculars.

PRISM TYPE. Binoculars are made with two types of prisms. Roof-prism binoculars have a straight barrel, so they're more compact. That makes them about 15% lighter—but they're also more expensive. Porro-prism binoculars, with the classic center dogleg, are bulkier but generally cost less.

FOCUS. Look for a fast-focus system with center focusing wheel that goes from infinity to near focus in one revolution or so. Extra-close focus is a real advantage for spotting perching birds. For birding, it's best to avoid self-focusing binoculars.

Test for smooth and even focusing. If you're considering waterproof binoculars, focusing may be stiff at first, but it will ease up with use.

SHOPPING TIPS. Make sure the binoculars give a clear, crisp, single image without warps or blurring. Look through the lenses toward a light source to be sure there's no prism effect around the edges of the image. Ask to try the binoculars outdoors. Also look for these features:

- With either roof- or porro-prism binoculars, multicoated lenses improve light transmission noticeably.

- If you wear glasses, roll-down or retractable rubber eye cups can improve viewing.

ROOF-PRISM BINOCULARS

Eyepiece

Focusing wheel

Prism

Objective lens   Light path

PORRO-PRISM BINOCULARS

Eyepiece

Prism

Focusing wheel

Objective lens   Light path

A male red-winged blackbird fluffs his feathers and displays his epaulets to win a mate and declare territorial rights.

BIRD BEHAVIOR

Whether birds are fluffing their feathers against the cold or flapping their wings in graceful flight, they make a garden seem more vibrantly alive. Observing their behavior will help you to identify which species have come to visit, feed, bathe, and perhaps build a nest on your property. Keeping a record of the specific behaviors adds greatly to the pleasure of bird-watching.

Besides helping you to distinguish a brown creeper from a winter wren, bird behavior marks the changing seasons. Once you've become familiar with patterns of behavior around the year, you can stay alert for migratory visitors or changing plumage.

BREEDING RITUALS. From courtship displays to intricate nest-making, birds' breeding behavior has evolved to ensure each species' reproductive success.

Claiming and defending a territory is the first challenge for many male birds. This territory, which may be as large as several acres or as small as a few suburban gardens, should provide food, water, and a secure nest site. Attracting a mate with song and display is the next order of business. Finally, the bird faces the task of protecting its territory, mate, and young from rivals of its own species and from predators.

Hummingbirds perform elaborate, sweeping courtship displays on the wing; these take the form of great aerial J, U, or O formations. The rhythmic drumming and exaggerated posturing of the downy woodpecker serve the same purpose. For most birds, these breeding rituals take place in the spring. But a few birds, like the mockingbird, hold and defend feeding territories year-round—which explains their aggressive behavior and unseasonal singing.

As spring progresses, you may see birds carrying nesting materials—perhaps a bit of grass or yarn, or some small twigs or even sticks. Each bird has its own distinctive style of construction, from the robin's cuplike mud-and-grass home to the bushtit's nest resembling a delicate sock of spiderweb, lichen, and grass. Thus the nest itself is a good clue to the bird's identity.

SURVIVAL SKILLS. After breeding, the focus of bird behavior shifts to simply staying alive. First and foremost is the search for food. Many birds have developed specialized skills to meet this task. The towhee scrapes the ground with both feet to unearth insects. The nuthatch travels head first down a tree trunk as it forages for bugs. And for many species, extraordinary feats of migratory flight are necessary to find enough food for survival (see page 82).

Between meals—and flights—all birds occasionally bathe, preen, or dust themselves. Fluffing feathers, huddling in a row, and tucking their heads under their wings are ways for birds to stay warm at night or in freezing weather. Some birds roost in large flocks; others keep to themselves.

Other kinds of behavior help birds to defend themselves against predators. Head bobbing is thought to help birds keep a sharp lookout from many angles. "Mobbing" is a group effort by birds of various species to harass a predator, such as a hawk, until it leaves.

READING RANGE MAPS

When interpreting range maps, keep in mind that the edges they show are often variable. Weather cycles and food supplies can have a major impact on where birds go and how they behave. Birds also have elevation ranges; if you're outside a species' elevation range, you are unlikely to see that bird even though you are within the general geographic area where it is found.

With several nestlings to feed, hunting for insects takes priority for a yellow warbler parent.

Putting on a convincing act to protect its young, a killdeer feigns a broken wing to lure intruders away from its nest.

A white-crowned sparrow launches into song.

TRILLS AND CHIRPS

A symbol of springtime and an inspiration for poets and composers, birdsong is far more than a free outdoor concert. For birds it is a basic way of communicating; for birders it's an identification tag to the various species.

Ornithologists divide bird sounds into two categories: songs and calls. Songs are the more melodious, complex strings of notes. But birds chirp—or "call"—at least as much as they sing, and for completely different purposes.

SONGS. As breeding season gets under way in spring, males sing to attract females—and to discourage intruders (usually males of the same species) from encroaching on their territory. The males, and sometimes the females, are apt to keep singing through the entire nesting cycle. In warm areas, this may begin as early as February and continue until July; songs diminish as fledglings leave the nest. Even species that sing all year long in some parts of the country (like the mockingbird) are more vocal during their breeding season.

CALLS. The brief, sharp chirps and squeaks birds make all year long are believed to serve less aggressive purposes than songs—perhaps warning of a predator, announcing that food is available, or simply keeping tabs on one another. The nasal chatter of

MIGRATORY VISITORS

Vast migrations of birds cross North America each spring and fall in one of the most amazing seasonal phenomena that a backyard birder can witness. A few of these migrants are likely to be attracted to your garden. Keep records over a period of years, and you'll see which ones use your yard for a day or perhaps a week in spring or fall—or even for a whole season. Eventually, you should be able to predict their arrival within a week or two.

Birds migrate through aerial corridors called flyways. Following coastlines, river systems, or mountain ranges, the primary North American routes are known as the Pacific, Central, Mississippi, and Atlantic flyways. But birds don't just fly north to south and back, but also east to west, over mountains and plains. They follow the course of a season's flower crop or an abundance of insect hatches. So, no matter where you live in North America, it's likely that migratory birds will drop by your garden occasionally. And bird banding shows that individual birds may return to the same backyard year after year throughout their life spans.

IN SEARCH OF GREENER PASTURES. Most birds migrate to seek food as it becomes unavailable where they live in winter. Actually, many migrant backyard birds are tropical species drawn to North America during their spring and summer breeding season by the food and nesting sites to be found here; in winter they simply fly back home.

As the face of our landscape has changed, so have migratory patterns. Whereas bird habitats might once have been isolated grasslands, forests, or deserts, the world has been vastly altered by farming, highway construction, and urbanization. Some habitats have been destroyed, at the expense of many species, and others created or opened up. Mockingbirds traveled northward with urbanization, which provided rooftops and low gardens similar to their original West Coast habitat on desert margins. Brewer's blackbirds and house finches expanded their ranges eastward as farms turned formerly inhospitable land into rich habitats.

The presence of cities across North America has also warmed certain climates just enough to allow small numbers of migratory species to cling to life in winter where they would otherwise not survive.

Gradually increasing numbers of migratory birds now remain far north of their 19th-century winter ranges as their red-breasted nuthatches as they flutter through a wooded lot, for example, keeps the flock together during its constant foraging.

For many small birds, these feeding and gathering calls are most likely to be heard in the morning and late afternoon. But at any time of day you might hear the excited calls of a mixed flock of woodpeckers, jays, chickadees, nuthatches, warblers, and finches joining to mob a Cooper's hawk or screech-owl. The raucous clatter will continue until the harassed predator flies off.

FINE-TUNING. Bird sounds can be a clue to identifying a species—but it takes some practice to sort out the various trills and twitters. And although sounds are consistent throughout some species, other species (like the white-crowned sparrow) encompass so much variation that the trained ear can detect two distinct local dialects in a single small city.

To complicate matters, jays, mockingbirds, and starlings specialize in mimicking other birds; even warblers and finches occasionally do so. Mimicry probably enhances a basic song to make it more attractive to females.

To develop your ear, look for tapes and CDs of bird songs at wildlife stores or order them from birders' catalogs and periodicals. Or else make your own tapes—a good cassette recorder and directional microphone are all you need.

needs are met by plantings and supplemental feedings in gardens across the continent. No species has abandoned migration entirely, but individual birds have learned to use certain garden plants, bird feeders, and birdbaths to survive through the winter.

Orioles were among the pioneers of this new pattern. Many thrushes, warblers, sparrows, blackbirds, and finches have also taken advantage of northern gardens.

FLIGHT FEATS. Some birds' migratory flights are incredible. The arctic tern traverses as many as 22,000 miles annually, flying from breeding grounds in arctic and subarctic North America, Asia, and Europe as far south as coastal Antarctica.

Many common backyard birds undertake marathon migrations, too. The barn swallow flies south to wintering grounds in Brazil and Argentina. Despite their delicate appearance, many hummingbirds that breed in the United States winter in Mexico, Central America, and South America. The tiny ruby-throated hummingbird is known to fly nonstop across the Gulf of Mexico.

Snow geese fly in formation, making their annual journey to breeding grounds in the Far North.

Various theories try to explain how migrating birds find their way across such long distances: Different species seem to use various environmental clues. Night-fliers may orient themselves by the stars or the earth's magnetic field. Birds that fly by day may use the sun, the magnetic field, or such landmarks as rivers, mountain ranges, or seacoasts to chart their course.

Birds normally fly no higher than 50 to 100 feet above the tops of trees. In migration they fly higher but still seldom exceed 1,000 feet. (Sightings have been made at 25,000 feet or higher.) Hawks, swifts, and swallows are among North America's highest flyers.

Most birds fly between 20 and 50 miles per hour, but in an emergency they can go faster. Peregrine falcons have been clocked at 175 miles per hour. Most birds are a lot slower than that, but they can still cover amazing distances in short periods of time. The migrating blackpoll warbler travels 30 to 200 miles each night, depending on the weather.

Once you've put out the welcome mat for birds, you'll want to be able to identify the avian guests that take advantage of your hospitality. Much of the enjoyment of hosting birds is in learning who's who and observing the particular characteristics of each kind of bird that comes to call.

A GARDEN
GUEST LIST

In the next 40 pages, you'll find descriptions of 84 species of birds that commonly appear in backyards and gardens across the continent—birds you might expect to see if you live within their range. A map for each species shows its typical North American range in winter, during the spring-summer breeding season, or all year.

Birds are grouped by families, in the order of their presumed ancestral relationships—from the "lowest" or most primitive to the "highest" or most recently evolved. This sequence, as well as English common names and Latin scientific names, is in keeping with the Check-list of North American Birds prepared by the American Ornithologists' Union. For more about bird families, see pages 74–75.

Of course, you'll see additional bird species in your area, too. To identify and read about them, consult a good field guide for North America or for your specific region.

American goldfinch pair alights on flowering Russian sage. By wintertime, the bright yellow breeding plumage of the male (below in photo) will fade to resemble the female's coloration.

AMERICAN KESTREL
(SPARROW HAWK)
Falco sparverius
FALCON FAMILY (FALCONIDAE)

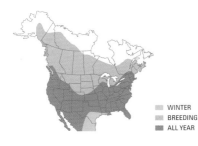

WINTER
BREEDING
ALL YEAR

Female kestrel

This robin-sized bird of prey with long, pointed wings is the smallest and most common falcon in North America. It has a reddish brown back and tail, overall black barring, and two vertical black stripes on each side of its white face; males (shown at right) are distinguished by slate blue wings and crown. Young birds look like males but are more heavily barred.

VOICE: The alarm call is a shrill, ringing *killy, killy, killy, killy.*

BEHAVIOR: Kestrels often sit on power lines or poles watching for prey or hover over grassy fields. Once prey is sighted, the little falcon folds its wings and dives, grasping its victim with its talons and carrying it to a nearby perch to consume it whole or in large pieces.

HABITAT: Open grasslands; common in cities, in suburbs, and along highways.

NATURAL FOOD: Insects, lizards, snakes, rodents (especially mice), and occasional songbirds.

NEST: Natural tree cavities or woodpecker holes are preferred as nest sites. The 4 or 5 eggs—white or light cinnamon, covered with small brown dots—are incubated for 29 to 31 days, mostly by the female. Young leave the nest about a month after hatching.

TO ATTRACT: Kestrels may nest in a birdhouse (8 by 8 by 14 inches high with a 3-inch entrance hole) raised 10 to 30 feet on a pole or tall tree in an open area. They may take finches or sparrows from feeders.

RING-NECKED PHEASANT
Phasianus colchicus
PHEASANT FAMILY (PHASIANIDAE)

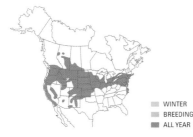

WINTER
BREEDING
ALL YEAR

A native of Asia, the ring-necked pheasant was introduced in North America more than a century ago and has done very well here. The 30- to 36-inch-long male is among the most spectacular of all birds, with its extravagant, multicolored, iridescent plumage, brilliant red face, green head, and long, tapering tail. The female is distinctly less showy, with buff plumage and a shorter tail.

VOICE: When flushed, the male cackles in alarm. A courting male crows like a rooster, then whirrs its wings.

BEHAVIOR: A male defends a breeding territory of a couple of acres against other males to win the right to mate with the three or four hens living there. To escape danger, a pheasant will usually run rather than fly.

HABITAT: Prairies, brushy fields, and cropland.

NATURAL FOOD: Grains from fields, weed seeds, berries from old fields; also insects in spring (such as grasshoppers, caterpillars, beetles).

NEST: The female makes a grassy nest on the ground in a natural hollow surrounded by protective vegetation; she incubates her 10 to 12 brownish buff eggs for 23 to 25 days. Chicks are able to leave the nest within a day.

TO ATTRACT: Offer seed at or near ground level. Pheasants like weedy garden edges near agricultural fields.

CALIFORNIA QUAIL
Callipepla californica
NEW WORLD QUAIL FAMILY
(ODONTOPHORIDAE)

WINTER
BREEDING
ALL YEAR

This sturdy-looking 10-inch bird looks much like the Gambel's quail (below), with its forehead plume, gray and brown coloration, and (in the male, pictured here) chestnut cap and white-edged black throat. What set the California quail apart are the scale-like markings across its belly and the brownish wash on its back.

VOICE: Calls range from *chi-ca-go* to assorted grunts.

BEHAVIOR: A courting male fluffs himself up, dips his wings, and spreads his tail to catch the female's attention. Outside the breeding season, these birds gather in coveys as large as 200, roosting in shrubs or low trees. They prefer to run rather than fly.

HABITAT: Scrubby, brushy areas near water; cultivated fields and suburbs.

NATURAL FOOD: Mainly seeds, also foliage and fruit; a few insects, spiders, and snails.

NEST: On the ground in a grass-lined depression under vegetation (or occasionally in a shrub), the female lays 12 to 16 creamy eggs with brownish markings. She incubates them for 21 to 23 days, and young fledge in 10 days.

TO ATTRACT: Seed will attract if there's sufficient cover nearby, as will water in ponds and birdbaths.

GAMBEL'S QUAIL
Callipepla gambelii
NEW WORLD QUAIL FAMILY
(ODONTOPHORIDAE)

WINTER
BREEDING
ALL YEAR

Short and rotund, the chickenlike gray Gambel's quail sports a teardrop-shaped plume on the forecrown. The 11-inch fowl has chestnut sides streaked with white. The male (shown in photo) has a black face and throat, a chestnut cap, and a black patch in the middle of his buff belly; the female is gray and brown.

VOICE: Calls vary from a loud *chi-ca-go-go* to grunts and chuckles used to locate other members of the flock.

BEHAVIOR: Like other quails, the Gambel's lives in coveys outside the breeding season. These flocks can total 40 or more birds, usually roosting in low shrubs at night—often near a water hole or creek to visit in early morning and late afternoon.

HABITAT: Dry or desert bottomland where scrub and sagebrush grow.

NATURAL FOOD: Mostly seeds, leaves, shoots, and buds of green desert plants; some insects and fruits.

NEST: The pair builds its nest of dry grasses on or near the ground under desert shrubs. The female incubates the 10 to 12 dull white to pale buff eggs, marked with brown, for 21 to 24 days. Chicks are almost immediately led from the nest, single file, by the male, with the female bringing up the rear.

TO ATTRACT: These desert birds frequent backyards and gardens offering water holes or birdbaths at ground level near abundant cover. They like birdseed, if cover is nearby.

NORTHERN BOBWHITE
Colinus virginianus
NEW WORLD QUAIL FAMILY
(ODONTOPHORIDAE)

WINTER
BREEDING
ALL YEAR

The classic "quail" of the East, this plump little fowl is a chickenlike 10-inch bird with a short tail and mottled red-brown coloring. The male (pictured) has a white throat and a white eye stripe; the female is all buff.

VOICE: The species gets its name from the bright *bob, bob-white* whistle the male often calls from a fence post in spring. A quiet *ka-loi-kee* call is uttered to assemble a family or covey.

BEHAVIOR: After the breeding season, several families join to form coveys, foraging by day and sleeping at night in a tight circle, tails toward the center. A threatened covey flushes, each bird flying out of the circle in the direction it's facing.

HABITAT: Farmland, open meadows, weedy pastures, open woodland.

NATURAL FOOD: Cropland grain and weed seeds most of the year, but also green shoots, insects, and berries in spring and summer.

NEST: A pair builds its nest on the ground under an arch of dead grasses. Both incubate the 14 to 16 creamy white eggs for 23 or 24 days. Chicks follow their parents from the nest within a day of hatching. Bobwhites produce at least 2 broods per year.

TO ATTRACT: Bobwhites appear regularly in yards where a birdseed mixture is spread on the ground. Weedy areas near thick cover may also attract them.

KILLDEER
Charadrius vociferus
PLOVER FAMILY (CHARADRIIDAE)

WINTER
BREEDING
ALL YEAR

The best-known member of the plover family, the killdeer is a 10-inch bird with a brown back and white belly interrupted by two distinct black bands (across upper breast and neck), a white collar, and a white spot above red-rimmed eyes. Its reddish rump and white wing bars show in flight. Male and female look alike.

VOICE: The killdeer is named for its familiar *kill-dee, kill-dee, kill-dee* call heard across open landscapes most of the year.

BEHAVIOR: To protect its nest or young from predators, an adult killdeer will convincingly feign a broken wing while calling a loud *trrrrrrrrr* to lure intruders away. On the ground, the birds typically run short distances, then stand still, then run again.

HABITAT: Often far from water and close to human habitation—roadsides, driveways, airports, cemeteries, parking lots, gravel roofs, and cultivated fields.

NATURAL FOOD: Mostly insects (about 98 percent of its diet), such as grasshoppers, beetles, ants, caterpillars, grubs, and spiders; also weed seeds gleaned from old fields.

NEST: The killdeer simply lays its 4 blotched brown oval eggs in a depression on open ground, usually amid gravel or debris. Both adults incubate the eggs for 24 to 26 days; chicks leave the nest as soon as they're dry. Two broods per year are common.

TO ATTRACT: Beaches and spacious graveled areas near water may attract killdeer as nesting sites.

Better known as a barn or city "pigeon," the 14-inch rock dove displays various color forms developed through domestication. Still, most resemble their wild ancestors—gray overall with darker heads, iridescent purple necks, and white rumps. Male and female look alike.

VOICE: The call is a soft *coo-a-roo, coo-ru-coooo, coo-a-coo.* A courting male coos while dancing before his mate.

BEHAVIOR: Rock doves were named for the attraction of the wild birds to rocks, cliffs, and ledges in their native European and Asian habitats; they have adapted in cities to the ledges of buildings, bridges, and monuments, and in the countryside to barn lofts and beams.

HABITAT: Buildings and other man-made structures in cities and suburbs.

NATURAL FOOD: Grains and green sprouts; also bread crumbs and garbage in cities.

NEST: Shallow and flimsy platform nests of grasses, straw, and other debris are built atop ledges and building beams and under bridges. Both adults share incubation of the 2 white eggs for 17 to 19 days. Young are in the nest more than a month before they can fly. Several broods per year are typical.

TO ATTRACT: Pigeons are eager but often unwanted seedeaters at urban feeding stations and water areas. They're messy, and they intimidate smaller birds.

ROCK DOVE
(PIGEON)
Columba livia
PIGEON AND DOVE FAMILY (COLUMBIDAE)

WINTER
BREEDING
ALL YEAR

A classic wild dove, this slender 12-inch bird (including its long, pointed tail) is gray-brown with scattered black spots and a pinkish wash on its breast. Male and female look alike except that in breeding plumage the male has a bluish crown (see photo). In flight, the tail shows white edges and the wings produce a whistle.

VOICE: Its melancholy *cwoo-ah, cwoo, cwoo, cwoo* call gives the mourning dove its common name. By counting males' coos in the spring, biologists can take a census of breeding pairs.

BEHAVIOR: This bird could have been called a "morning" dove—it is most active between 7 and 9 A.M. The young are fed "pigeon milk," a granular fluid produced in the adult crop and pumped directly into nestlings' mouths by both male and female.

HABITAT: Urban and suburban gardens, farms, and parks throughout North America, especially near water.

NATURAL FOOD: Almost entirely grains and seeds of weeds and grasses, eaten at ground level.

NEST: A flimsy nest of sticks built in a tree supports 2 white eggs, incubated by both parents for 13 or 14 days. Young leave the nest 2 weeks after hatching. A pair may produce 2 to 5 broods each summer.

TO ATTRACT: Mourning doves are easily attracted by offering cracked corn and smaller grains in tray feeders on or near the ground. Water also entices, as do coniferous trees in which to nest.

MOURNING DOVE
Zenaida macroura
PIGEON AND DOVE FAMILY (COLUMBIDAE)

WINTER
BREEDING
ALL YEAR

Quails, Plovers, and Doves **89**

WESTERN AND EASTERN SCREECH-OWL

Otus kennicottii, Otus asio
OWL FAMILY (STRIGIDAE)

Western screech-owl   Eastern screech-owl

■ WINTER ■ BREEDING ■ ALL YEAR

At 9 inches, the screech-owl is one of the smallest owls with ear tufts in North America. The eastern screech-owl can be either mottled gray or red; the western species is usually gray with a darker bill. Male and female look just the same.

VOICE: Despite the name, screech-owls don't screech. The eastern owl utters a tremulous, eerie cry in the night. The western species emits a rhythmic series of whistles.

Western screech-owl   Eastern screech-owl

BEHAVIOR: These nocturnal birds can often be seen sitting in the entrances of tree cavities or birdhouses at dusk, half asleep. Hunting begins soon after dark.

HABITAT: Forests, farm woodlots, and shade trees in backyards and parks.

NATURAL FOOD: Mice, shrews, large insects, small reptiles, amphibians, songbirds, small game birds, and small birds of prey—including other screech-owls.

NEST: These cavity nesters will appropriate woodpecker holes and large birdhouses as places in which to lay their 4 or 5 pure white eggs. The female incubates the eggs for 21 to 30 days while the male brings her food. Youngsters leave the nest a month later.

TO ATTRACT: Position a large birdhouse (8 by 8 by 14 inches high with a 3-inch entrance hole) 10 to 30 feet high in a mature tree, such as a large oak. Dead trees provide nest sites, too. Screech-owls will drink and bathe in garden ponds at night.

GREAT HORNED OWL

Bubo virginianus
OWL FAMILY (STRIGIDAE)

■ WINTER
■ BREEDING
■ ALL YEAR

The 22-inch great horned owl is a striking bird with ear tufts, mottled brown plumage, and a white throat. Male and female look the same.

VOICE: The great horned's 4 to 6 deep hoots—*whoo-whoo-whoo-whoo-whoo*—can be heard throughout the year but are most common in fall and winter.

BEHAVIOR: Considered the ultimate predator by many, this owl has extremely sensitive hearing and swoops down on its prey on silent wings, attacking with powerful talons. The presence of these owls is most noticeable at night, when they hoot.

HABITAT: Deep forests, second-growth forests, deserts, rural areas, and small towns throughout North America.

NATURAL FOOD: A variety of prey—skunks, rats, weasels, domestic cats, large snakes, squirrels, chipmunks, woodchucks, rabbits, game birds (such as pheasant, grouse, and waterfowl), and other birds of prey (including other owl species).

NEST: No native species nests earlier—February in many areas, even earlier in warmer regions of the South. A pair may use the large nest of a hawk, eagle, crow, or heron or a large tree cavity, stump, or rock ledge as a nest site. The 2 dull white eggs require about 30 days of incubation, mostly by the female. Young don't leave the nest for at least 2 months.

TO ATTRACT: These owls will live in any yard with mature habitat that supports a variety of wildlife, especially a grove of tall conifers.

Bow-shaped wings are the signature of the 5-inch chimney swift, the only swift found east of the Mississippi River. Both male and female are dark gray with lighter throats. In flight, stiff wing beats distinguish these birds from similar-looking swallows.

VOICE: The chimney swift emits loud, high-pitched chipperings as it flutters overhead.

BEHAVIOR: Rarely seen perched or at its nest, this swift is almost always observed flying above cities and suburbs on summer evenings. In winter, the entire population migrates to the Amazon River basin.

HABITAT: Formerly hollow trees and caves, but nowadays the open air above cities, towns, villages, and farms—anywhere chimneys are available.

NATURAL FOOD: Insects caught during flight.

NEST: As its name suggests, this bird nests in chimneys—and in air shafts, attics, silos, and old wells. The pair attaches its twig nest to the wall with saliva (like the nest of the related Asian swift of bird's-nest soup fame). The 4 or 5 pure white oval eggs are incubated by both parents, sometimes at the same time, for 18 to 21 days. Young fly when they're a month old but may return to the nest to roost.

TO ATTRACT: Any urban or suburban chimney within the bird's range is a potential nesting site.

CHIMNEY SWIFT
Chaetura pelagica
SWIFT FAMILY (APODIDAE)

WINTER
BREEDING
ALL YEAR

Of all the hummingbirds breeding in the United States and Canada, only the ruby-throated nests east of the Great Plains. Male and female alike are 3- to 3½-inch flying jewels with iridescent metallic green bodies and long, needle-sharp bills. The fork-tailed male (pictured at left) sports a fiery red iridescent throat; the female (below with nestlings) is gray-white below and has a blunted tail.

VOICE: Both sexes utter high-pitched, squeaky chippering calls and make buzzing noises with their wings. Males buzz during pendulum-patterned courtship flights.

BEHAVIOR: Like all hummingbirds, ruby-throats spend a great deal of time on the wing, buzzing here and there in search of flowers containing nectar. When they do shut down their motors, they often perch inconspicuously on tree branches.

HABITAT: Gardens surrounded by woodland vegetation, orchards, or shade trees.

NATURAL FOOD: Mostly flower nectar; also tiny insects and spiders.

NEST: The female uses spider silk to attach her tiny, cup-shaped nest to a small twig or branch 6 to 50 feet above the ground. Lined with plant down, the nest usually contains 2 white eggs the size of navy beans. The female incubates them for 14 to 16 days; young leave in about 3 weeks.

TO ATTRACT: Ruby-throats are attracted by brightly colored, nectar-producing flowers in gardens surrounded by trees. They also drink sugar water.

RUBY-THROATED HUMMINGBIRD
Archilochus colubris
HUMMINGBIRD FAMILY (TROCHILIDAE)

WINTER
BREEDING
ALL YEAR

BLACK-CHINNED HUMMINGBIRD

Archilochus alexandri
HUMMINGBIRD FAMILY (TROCHILIDAE)

WINTER
BREEDING
ALL YEAR

A black chin above a bluish purple throat distinguishes the male black-chinned hummingbird. Both sexes of this 3½-inch bird are metallic green above; the female is white below. The male (pictured) has a notched tail.

VOICE: The male sings a soft, high-pitched *chew*. When chasing other hummers, it makes a loud chippering sound.

BEHAVIOR: Like its close relative the ruby-throated hummingbird, the black-chinned male courts females with a dramatic pendulum flight, sometimes tracing a figure eight.

HABITAT: Semiarid canyons and woodlands near streams, lowlands, and parks.

NATURAL FOOD: The pollen and nectar of tree flowers and garden blossoms; also insects captured by darting out from a tree perch.

NEST: Typically, the small, cup-shaped nest is built by the female 4 to 8 feet up in a tree or shrub, using white or buff plant down covered with spider silk. Two pure white eggs are incubated by the female for about 16 days. Young leave the nest about 3 weeks after hatching but are still fed by the female; 2 or 3 broods per year are common.

TO ATTRACT: Western gardens with native plants producing small, bright-colored, nectar-filled flowers should attract these hummers. Surrounding woodlands draw them—as does sugar water.

ANNA'S HUMMINGBIRD

Calypte anna
HUMMINGBIRD FAMILY (TROCHILIDAE)

WINTER
BREEDING
ALL YEAR

A mong the most spectacular of North American hummingbirds, the 4-inch Anna's has a jewel-like metallic green body—punctuated in the male with a brilliant iridescent rose forehead and throat (see photo). The female lacks the bright top but usually has some rose-colored throat feathers.

VOICE: The male sings a series of thin, squeaky notes from a tree perch or while in a courtship flight. Both sexes chirp while feeding from blossoms.

BEHAVIOR: This is one hummingbird species that often winters in the United States. During the summer breeding season, the female may build a new nest, lay eggs, and begin to incubate while still feeding youngsters from the previous brood. In warmer areas, nesting may begin as early as December.

HABITAT: Chaparral, mixed woodlands, parks, and gardens.

NATURAL FOOD: Insects (more than most other hummingbirds), bleeding tree sap from sapsucker drillings, and the nectar of tree blossoms and garden flowers.

NEST: Somewhat large for a hummingbird nest, the cup of plant down covered with spider silk and lichens is built on a branch as high as 30 feet above ground. The 2 white eggs are incubated by the female for 16 days. Young fly in about 3 weeks.

TO ATTRACT: Sugar-water feeders in a flower garden featuring nectar-filled blooms, surrounded by natural habitat, should bring the Anna's.

Similar in appearance to the ruby-throated (see page 91), the male of the 4½-inch broad-tailed hummingbird species has a rosy red throat, white belly, and metallic green body (see photo). The female is green above with a speckled throat and reddish brown flanks and belly.

VOICE: The call is a sharp *chip,* but a more characteristic noise is the loud, musical, cricketlike buzzing of the male's wings in flight.

BEHAVIOR: Like other hummingbirds, the broad-tail is an incredible flier, zipping up and down, back and forth, or hanging in midair while its wings beat in a blur.

HABITAT: Forests of piñon and juniper, canyons, and gardens in the Rocky Mountain region at elevations of 4,000 to 11,000 feet.

NATURAL FOOD: Nectar and insects found on and around high-country vegetation.

NEST: The female builds her nest 3 to 20 feet up on a horizontal branch of a tree or shrub. Tree down forms the outer walls of the cup, which is decorated with shreds of bark, fine leaves, and lichen. The 2 white eggs are incubated by the female for 16 days; young are on the wing in about 3 weeks.

TO ATTRACT: The broad-tail sips nectar from red geraniums, penstemons, lupines, petunias, and other bright flowers (especially natives). It drinks sugar water and is attracted to hummingbird feeders in summer.

BROAD-TAILED HUMMINGBIRD
Selasphorus platycercus
HUMMINGBIRD FAMILY (TROCHILIDAE)

WINTER
BREEDING
ALL YEAR

A totally red head is the main distinguishing feature of both the male and female red-headed woodpecker. This bird is very showy in flight as its black-and-white back, wings, and tail ripple through the woods.

The introduction of the European starling in North America in the late 19th century created unnatural competition for nesting cavities. That and loss of habitat have made the red-headed woodpecker scarce in the northeastern United States.

VOICE: Its *queeah, queeah, queeah* call is often heard before this bird is seen.

BEHAVIOR: The red-headed doesn't drill trees for food as much as other woodpeckers do, foraging instead on the ground for ants, spiders, grubs, wasps, and beetles.

HABITAT: Mature woodlands of both coniferous and deciduous forests, wooded farmlands, and city parks and gardens in the East and Midwest.

NATURAL FOOD: Animal matter; also tree nuts and the fruits and seeds of trees, shrubs, and vines.

NEST: Male and female share excavation of their 8- to 24 inch-deep nesting cavity, usually 8 to 80 feet above the ground in a live or dead tree, utility pole, or fence post. The 5 pure white eggs are incubated by both male and female for about 14 days. Young can fly in about a month.

TO ATTRACT: If you have mature trees nearby, offer suet and birdseed to attract this woodpecker. It may nest in a birdhouse (6 by 6 by 14 inches high with a 2-inch hole) erected 12 to 20 feet above the ground. Dead trees provide nest sites, too.

RED-HEADED WOODPECKER
Melanerpes erythrocephalus
WOODPECKER FAMILY (PICIDAE)

WINTER
BREEDING
ALL YEAR

RED-BELLIED WOODPECKER

Melanerpes carolinus
WOODPECKER FAMILY (PICIDAE)

WINTER
BREEDING
ALL YEAR

The zebra-backed, 9-inch male red-bellied woodpecker has a bright red crown and nape, a white rump, and white patches on the outer wings (see photo). The female is similar, but only her nape is red. Red-bellied woodpeckers do have a reddish wash on the lower belly, but it's difficult to see.

VOICE: The distinct *yuk* call, once learned, is easily recognized. The red-bellied also calls a series of *chuf-chuf-chuf-chuf* notes.

BEHAVIOR: Originally a southeastern species, the red-bellied has extended its range as far as New England and the Midwest, thanks in part to feeding stations.

HABITAT: Forests, orchards, gardens, and backyards with mature trees.

NATURAL FOOD: Wood-boring insects, beetles, crickets, and flies; acorns and other nuts that can be cached for winter use. Citrus fruits and juice are favorites, too.

NEST: Male and female dig a nesting cavity 5 to 70 feet above the ground in a tree, utility pole, or building. The 4 or 5 pure white eggs are incubated by both for 14 days, and young are on the wing in 3½ weeks.

TO ATTRACT: Suet, sunflower seeds, and cracked corn will attract this woodpecker. It may use a birdhouse (6 by 6 by 14 inches high with a 2½-inch hole) placed 12 to 20 feet high. Dead trees also provide nest sites.

YELLOW-BELLIED SAPSUCKER

Sphyrapicus varius
WOODPECKER FAMILY (PICIDAE)

WINTER
BREEDING
ALL YEAR

This multicolored 8-inch woodpecker has a bright red forehead, black-and-white head, long white wing bar, and black barred back. Its yellowish belly has some speckling. The male (pictured) has a red throat; the female, a white throat. In some regions, the yellow-bellied has more red on the head—like its close relatives the red-naped sapsucker of the Rockies and the red-breasted sapsucker of the Pacific Coast.

VOICE: A nasal *mew* and the alarm cry *churr-churr-churr* are common calls.

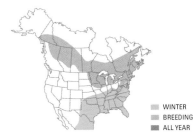

BEHAVIOR: This sapsucker doesn't actually suck sap, but the holes it drills in trees make the sap run, enabling the bird to lap it up with its brushlike tongue. It returns to the holes to harvest insects attracted to the sap.

HABITAT: Coniferous or deciduous forests; wooded groves around homes and gardens.

NATURAL FOOD: Tree sap and the insects attracted to the sap; other woodland insects.

NEST: A nesting cavity 10 to 12 inches deep is excavated by male and female in a live or dead tree, 5 to 30 feet high. On average, 4 eggs are incubated by both parents (the male at night) for 11 or 12 days. The youngsters leave the nest in about a month.

TO ATTRACT: Yellow-bellieds love suet and also relish the sugar water in hummingbird feeders. They like to drill holes in deciduous fruit trees.

WINTER
BREEDING
ALL YEAR

The male downy is a little black-and-white woodpecker with a single red spot on the back of its head (see photo). The female lacks the red spot. This 6-inch bird has a short bill, and its outer tailfeathers are usually barred.

VOICE: A high-pitched whinny is the location call; a contented *pik,* the feeding call.

BEHAVIOR: During winter, both sexes begin drumming on trees to establish nesting territories. In late winter, courting pairs dance around tree branches, wings raised in tempo with the birds' chattering.

HABITAT: Open woodlands of mixed growth, orchards, swamps, riverbanks, and wooded backyards.

NATURAL FOOD: Wood-boring insects, insect eggs, and cocoons; also fruits, weed seeds, and crop grains. Clinging to a tree, a downy pecks with jerking movements to scale away loose bark in search of food.

NEST: The female does most of the work excavating the nest, an 8- to 10-inch-deep tree cavity 3 to 50 feet above the ground. Both parents incubate the 4 or 5 white eggs (the male at night) for 12 days; the young are on the wing in about 3 weeks.

TO ATTRACT: Of all woodpeckers, this is the most common visitor to backyards across the continent—especially those with fruit trees. It's fond of suet but will also eat cracked sunflower seeds and corn. Dead trees are attractive as nest sites.

HAIRY WOODPECKER
Picoides villosus
WOODPECKER FAMILY (PICIDAE)

WINTER
BREEDING
ALL YEAR

Except for its larger size, the 9-inch hairy woodpecker is almost a copy of the downy (above). Its bill is also larger and more chiseled, and its outer tailfeathers show no barring. Bristlelike feathers around the bill give this woodpecker its name.

VOICE: The hairy's whinny is deeper and faster than the downy's, and its *peek* call is louder and more metallic.

BEHAVIOR: Hairy woodpeckers are much shyer than downies. Once they settle on a breeding territory, a pair is likely to remain there for the rest of their lives.

HABITAT: Coniferous and deciduous forests, swamps, and orchards—and backyards that have mature trees.

NATURAL FOOD: The larvae of wood-boring insects make up more than 75 percent of the diet. It is believed that a hairy can actually hear or feel the insects with its bill when it pecks into a tree.

NEST: A new nesting cavity is built each year, 10 to 12 inches deep and 5 to 30 feet above the ground, often in a tree with a decayed center. The 4 white eggs are incubated by both sexes (the male at night) for 11 or 12 days. Young birds are out of the nest in about a month.

TO ATTRACT: Suet is the major food attractant, but sunflower seeds, corn, and scraps of meat and fruit will also be eaten. Dead trees provide nest sites.

NORTHERN FLICKER
Colaptes auratus
WOODPECKER FAMILY (PICIDAE)

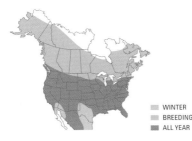

WINTER
BREEDING
ALL YEAR

The flicker is a large woodpecker—12 inches long—with a brown striped back and a spotted, buff-colored belly. Both sexes have black bibs and white rumps, but only the males have "mustaches"—either black (in the East) or red (in the West). Regional forms also vary in the color of their wing feather shafts: yellow in the East and red in the West. These differences show up best in flight. Eastern (yellow-shafted) flickers of both sexes have a red chevron on the nape, not present in western birds.

VOICE: Flickers are loud birds, and their rhythmic call—*ka-ka-ka-ka*—can often be heard at a great distance.

BEHAVIOR: Northern flickers are unique among woodpeckers because they feed on the ground rather than in trees.

HABITAT: Open deciduous and coniferous forests, orchards, roadsides, backyard lawns.

NATURAL FOOD: Ants and other ground-inhabiting insects, procured by means of the flicker's long, sticky tongue; also fruit, berries, and weed seeds.

NEST: Flickers nest in tree cavities 2 to 60 feet above the ground; both sexes help to excavate the nest to a depth of 10 to 36 inches. The 6 to 8 white eggs are incubated for 11 or 12 days, mostly by the male. Young are out of the nest in less than a month.

TO ATTRACT: Northern flickers like suet, raisins and apples. They might nest in a birdhouse 7 by 7 by 18 inches high with a 2½-inch hole, erected 6 to 20 feet high. Dead trees provide nest sites, too.

BLACK PHOEBE
Sayornis nigricans
FLYCATCHER FAMILY (TYRANNIDAE)

WINTER
BREEDING
ALL YEAR

The black phoebe looks similar to the dark-eyed junco (page 117), but its erect posture and flicking tail distinguish it as a member of the flycatcher family. The 7-inch bird is black overall (both male and female) except for a white lower belly, undertail coverts, and outer tail feathers.

VOICE: The song is a high-pitched, plaintive *ti-wee*, sounded twice; the alarm note is a loud, sharp *tsip*.

BEHAVIOR: This bird of the shadows watches for insect prey from a shaded perch, attacking from above on mothlike wings. The clicking of its bill indicates a strike.

HABITAT: Always near water—along shaded streams, on farms, and in parks and gardens.

NATURAL FOOD: Wasps, flies, ants, moths, and caterpillars.

NEST: The mud nest is built over doors and windows, under bridges, and on cliffs, often under an overhang, sometimes near heavy human traffic, and always near water. A lining of wool, hair, feathers, or plant fibers cushions 4 white eggs, incubated by the female for 15 to 17 days; 3 weeks later the young can fly.

TO ATTRACT: If you've seen black phoebes nearby, you might provide a shelf in a place where the birds could nest. A pool or damp lawn also attracts them.

The 6½-inch eastern phoebe—male and female alike—is dark olive above, with a slightly darker head, and whitish below. Like other flycatchers, this bird sits upright, flipping its tail.

VOICE: The eastern phoebe calls its name with a distinct *fee-bee, fee-bee,* repeated over and over again.

BEHAVIOR: The eastern phoebe is one of the earliest birds to migrate north to its nesting grounds in the spring; it also lingers there longer in the fall.

WINTER
BREEDING
ALL YEAR

HABITAT: Near man-made structures close to water in ravines, around cliffs, and in suburban areas.

NATURAL FOOD: Almost entirely insects, usually caught in flight.

NEST: On a shelflike projection over a window, on rafters of a barn or outbuilding, or on bridge girders, a 4½-inch nest is built of weeds, grasses, plant fibers, and mud, then covered with moss and lined with hair; 5 white eggs, on the average, are incubated by the female for 15 or 16 days. Young leave 2 to 3 weeks later. Two broods per year are common. Brown-headed cowbirds (page 122) often remove phoebe eggs from the nest and replace them with their own.

TO ATTRACT: Build a shelf onto a building in an area inhabited by phoebes; the birds will likely nest there. A pond or small lake will also attract them.

This rather nondescript 6-inch-long bird is olive green above and white below, with a gray cap. Above its red eye is a white stripe topped with a black line. Both sexes look the same.

VOICE: The male's song seems to go on and on forever with the same *See me. Here I am. Don't you see me? Here I am.* Its scolding note is a harsh, nasal *nyeah.*

BEHAVIOR: The red-eyed vireo throws its voice like a ventriloquist and is therefore difficult to locate in dense foliage.

HABITAT: Open deciduous forests with thick understories of saplings.

NATURAL FOOD: Insects gleaned in the foliage of deciduous trees, including some that are harmful to the trees. Moths and caterpillars are favorites.

NEST: Like the birds themselves, the cup-shaped nest is well hidden, hanging from a fork of a horizontal branch 5 to 10 feet above the ground. Using grasses, rootlets, bark strips, and paper, the female builds the nest in about 5 days, then lays 4 white, slightly spotted eggs and incubates them for 12 to 14 days. Young birds fly from the nest in another 10 to 12 days.

TO ATTRACT: Offer moving water in a wooded habitat with native deciduous trees.

RED-EYED VIREO
Vireo olivaceus
VIREO FAMILY (VIREONIDAE)

WINTER
BREEDING
ALL YEAR

Woodpeckers, Flycatchers, and Vireos 97

STELLER'S JAY
Cyanocitta stelleri
CROW AND JAY FAMILY (CORVIDAE)

WINTER
BREEDING
ALL YEAR

The all-blue crested Steller's jay of the West is a 12-inch bird with dark blue wings and tail; black markings on the head, upper back, and breast; and inconspicuous white streaks on the face. Male and female look alike.

VOICE: This is a loud bird, squawking *waah, waah, waah* and *shook, shook, shook,* but during courtship, the male whispers his song to his mate. The Steller's jay mimics the voices of red-shouldered and red-tailed hawks.

BEHAVIOR: Often shy in deep forests, the Steller's can be bold at campsites and picnic grounds. Although it may travel in flocks of a dozen or more, it's less gregarious than other jays (but more so than the scrub-jay). Parents are quiet near their nest but protest loudly if discovered.

HABITAT: Western coniferous forests and mixed oak-pine woodlands.

NATURAL FOOD: Acorns and pine seeds that can be hoarded for winter consumption; also insects, eggs and young of small birds, carrion, and camp leftovers. The Steller's will sometimes raid woodpeckers' acorn stores and the caches of other jays.

NEST: Eight to 40 feet up in a tree (usually a conifer), the pair builds its bulky nest of dry leaves, moss, and trash mixed with mud, lining it with rootlets and pine needles. The 4 pale greenish eggs, spotted brown, are incubated primarily by the female for 17 or 18 days.

TO ATTRACT: Steller's jays like the moist shade of conifers; birdseed, peanuts, and suet are favorite foods.

BLUE JAY
Cyanocitta cristata
CROW AND JAY FAMILY (CORVIDAE)

WINTER
BREEDING
ALL YEAR

The East's blue-crested jay is a striking 11-inch bird that's bright blue above, with white on its wings and tail, and light gray below. Both sexes look alike.

VOICE: The demanding *jay, jay, jay* can be heard at some distance. The bell-like *too-lee, too-lee* call is softer. The male's whisper song is for his mate. Blue jays mimic the calls of red-shouldered and red-tailed hawks.

BEHAVIOR: The blue jay is aggressive and crafty. During courtship, several males will chase a single female until she selects one of them as a mate.

HABITAT: Forests, farms, parks, and the backyards and gardens of suburbs and cities.

NATURAL FOOD: Acorns and other tree seeds and nuts; also grains, fruits, insects, fish, salamanders, sometimes small birds, and eggs in nests.

NEST: Bulky nests are well hidden in thickets, frequently near houses, 5 to 50 feet above the ground. Both male and female gather sticks, twigs, bark, and leaves for the nest and line it with rootlets; both incubate the 4 or 5 eggs (olive or buff-colored with dark brown spots) for 17 or 18 days. Youngsters fly in about 3 weeks.

TO ATTRACT: Just offer peanuts, sunflower and other seeds, suet, and water.

A crestless jay that's bright blue above and light gray below, the western scrub-jay has a distinct white eyebrow, white throat, and blue breast band. Nearly half of its slender 11-inch body is tail. Male and female look alike.

VOICE: The western scrub-jay utters a harsh *shreep, shreep, shreep.* The male also whispers a quieter song to his mate.

BEHAVIOR: Bold and tame around backyards and gardens, these jays often cache food and have been known to steal bright, shiny objects—such as pieces of glass or jewelry.

HABITAT: Scrub oaks, mesquite woodlands, deserts, canyons, stream bottomlands.

NATURAL FOOD: Acorns, pine nuts, other tree seeds, grains, fruits, insects, snails, and the eggs and young of small birds. Western scrub-jays spend much of their time foraging on the ground for food.

NEST: A low nesting site, 3 to 30 feet above ground in a bush or shrub, is typical. The

WINTER
BREEDING
ALL YEAR

scrub-jay's nest is a well-constructed cup of twigs, moss, and dry grass lined with hair and rootlets. The 3 or 4 greenish eggs marked with brown spots are incubated by the female for about 16 days. Young leave the nest 2 or 3 weeks later.

TO ATTRACT: These birds will become faithful visitors to backyards that offer beef suet, birdseed, or peanuts.

The American crow is entirely black for the length of its 18-inch body, from its squared-off tail to its bill. Even its feet are black.

VOICE: The crow's hoarse *caw, caw, caw* is a familiar sound on farms across the continent. Young crows in the nest are noisy, with a more nasal call.

BEHAVIOR: Considered among the most intelligent of all birds, the crow can learn quickly and communicate complicated information to its fellow crows.

HABITAT: Forests, farmlands, wooded lots, and suburban areas with mature trees.

NATURAL FOOD: Nearly anything—carrion on highways, fish, earthworms, insects, and the eggs and young of other birds, as well as fruit, grains, and garbage.

AMERICAN CROW
Corvus brachyrhynchos
CROW AND JAY FAMILY (CORVIDAE)

WINTER
BREEDING
ALL YEAR

NEST: A pair usually builds its large, basketlike nest of sticks 10 to 70 feet up in a tree or shrub, lining it with shredded bark, moss, feathers, fur, hair, roots, or leaves. Both parents incubate the 4 to 6 bluish or grayish green eggs, spotted brown, for 18 days. Young fly when they're about a month old.

TO ATTRACT: Most people don't try to attract crows—they can be destructive to other birds and crops—but they'll come for suet and birdseed.

PURPLE MARTIN
Progne subis
SWALLOW FAMILY
(HIRUNDINIDAE)

WINTER
BREEDING
ALL YEAR

A t 8 inches, the purple martin is the largest American swallow. The male (shown below) is glossy blue-black overall; the female (pictured at gourd house) and immature birds are duller above, with gray bellies and mottled throats. All have forked tails.

VOICE: With wings outstretched, the purple martin calls a harsh *keerp*. Its song is a gurgling, liquid sound ending with a series of guttural notes.

BEHAVIOR: Colonies return every spring, on about the same date, to where they hatched. An advance guard of several males is joined a few days later by the main flock.

HABITAT: Open areas near water—on farms, in cities, and in suburbs—where they can swoop down from their houses to feed on insects.

NATURAL FOOD: Insects, including mosquitoes and dragonflies.

NEST: Ever since Native Americans hollowed out gourds for purple martins, they've been nesting in man-made houses. Today, thousands of multiple-room martin houses are erected on lawns and in gardens across the continent. Only in the West do the birds still nest in natural cavities. Each pair produces 4 or 5 white eggs, which the female incubates for 15 or 16 days; young are ready to fly in about a month.

TO ATTRACT: Erect a multiple-room martin house 15 to 20 feet above ground on a pole in an open area near water. Dead trees may be used as nest sites, too.

TREE SWALLOW
Tachycineta bicolor
SWALLOW FAMILY (HIRUNDINIDAE)

WINTER
BREEDING
ALL YEAR

T he first swallow to move north in the spring, the handsome 5- to 6-inch tree swallow is steely blue-green above and white below. Male (pictured) and female are similar, but females are much browner. Young birds are brownish gray above and white below with a shaded breast band.

VOICE: The liquid, twittering song is a pleasant chatter. In flight, the bird will call *silip*.

BEHAVIOR: Unlike some swallows, these are not colonial birds and usually nest in isolated pairs. They do flock during migration, when their numbers can be impressive.

HABITAT: Wooded swamps or open fields near water but often close to humans.

NATURAL FOOD: Mostly insects taken in flight while the bird courses over water or fields; some weed seeds and fruits as well.

NEST: These cavity nesters will use holes in trees, birdhouses, mailboxes, and fence posts. The nest itself is an accumulation of grasses lined with feathers; 4 to 6 pure white eggs are incubated for 13 to 16 days by the female. Young leave the nest in about 3 weeks, or whenever conditions are favorable.

TO ATTRACT: Place birdhouses (5 by 5 by 6 inches high, with a 1½-inch diameter hole) 10 to 15 feet high on posts near water.

The male violet-green swallow has a brilliant green back and purple rump, white belly, and notched tail (see photo). The female is browner above, and young birds are gray. Similar to the tree swallow, this 5½-inch western species has more white on its flanks, nearly meeting over the tail and also surrounding the eye.

VOICE: Violet-greens twitter a great deal while in flight. The male sings *tsip-tseet-tsip* while courting.

BEHAVIOR: This bird seems to enjoy flying high, chattering as it flutters in search of insects.

HABITAT: Open woodlands along the Pacific Coast and at higher elevations in the mountains, north to Alaska.

NATURAL FOOD: Insects taken on the wing, often at great heights.

NEST: Though they frequently nest in single pairs, violet-greens will sometimes nest near tree swallows, bluebirds, nuthatches, woodpeckers, and wrens in wooded areas where there are lots of holes. They build their nests in natural cavities, old woodpecker holes, cliffs, or birdhouses, using dried grasses and feathers as lining. The 4 or 5 oval white eggs are incubated by the female for 13 or 14 days. Young fly 10 days after hatching but may return to roost.

TO ATTRACT: If you live in the West near water, try erecting a birdhouse (5 by 5 by 6 inches high with a 1½-inch diameter hole) 10 to 15 feet high on a post.

VIOLET-GREEN SWALLOW
Tachycineta thalassina
SWALLOW FAMILY (HIRUNDINIDAE)

WINTER
BREEDING
ALL YEAR

The barn swallow is the most common and best-known member of its family in North America; its most distinctive feature is a dramatically forked tail—the classic "swallow tail." Both male and female are metallic blue-black above and creamy white to cinnamon below, with a darker reddish brown throat. Young barn swallows are paler below and have shorter tails.

VOICE: The barn swallow chatters constantly, stringing together a variety of harsh notes.

BEHAVIOR: Barn swallows are superb fliers, always making aerial adjustments as they search for insects and court mates. They drink and bathe while skimming ponds.

HABITAT: Barns, natural caves, outbuildings, bridges, and other structures on farms and in suburbs.

NATURAL FOOD: Insects taken on the wing over fields, meadows, barnyards, ponds.

NEST: These colonial birds often plaster their mud nests to rafters or beams of barns, bridges, or boathouses. On a lining of feathers, the 4 or 5 brown-spotted white eggs are incubated by both parents—sometimes alternating every 15 minutes—for 15 days. The female sits on the eggs at night while the male stays nearby. Young fly in about 3 weeks.

TO ATTRACT: Barn swallows seem to adopt people; people don't adopt them. But you can invite them by constructing a narrow ledge in the rafters or corner of a building. They love ponds and need mud for their nests.

BARN SWALLOW
Hirundo rustica
SWALLOW FAMILY (HIRUNDINIDAE)

WINTER
BREEDING
ALL YEAR

BLACK-CAPPED CHICKADEE

Poecile atricapillus
CHICKADEE AND TITMOUSE
FAMILY (PARIDAE)

WINTER
BREEDING
ALL YEAR

A gray and black ball of fluff weighing just ⅓ of an ounce—that's the black-capped chickadee. Gray above and whitish below, this 5-inch bird is distinguished by a distinct black cap, a black bib, white cheek marks, buff-colored flanks, and a long tail. Male and female look alike.

VOICE: A more definitive identification might be the *chick-a-dee-dee-dee* call, or the male's springtime *phee-bee* song.

BEHAVIOR: This active, curious, and quick-moving bird can change directions in midair in ³⁄₁₀₀ of a second. It's among the tamest of all backyard species and can even be trained to eat from the hand.

HABITAT: Deciduous and coniferous forests, rural woodlands, and suburban backyards in the northern United States.

NATURAL FOOD: The eggs and larvae of tree-inhabiting insects; also fruit and seeds.

NEST: Both sexes excavate the 5- to 8-inch nesting cavity in rotting wood, 4 to 10 feet above the ground. During the 12 to 13 days the female incubates the 6 to 8 eggs (white with reddish brown spots), the male feeds her. Both feed the young during the 2-week nesting period.

TO ATTRACT: Black-capped chickadees love sunflower seeds. They may nest in a birdhouse (4 by 4 by 10 inches high with a 1¼-inch entrance hole) placed 6 to 15 feet high; they'll also nest in dead trees. They like coniferous shrubs and trees.

CAROLINA CHICKADEE

Poecile carolinensis
CHICKADEE AND TITMOUSE FAMILY
(PARIDAE)

WINTER
BREEDING
ALL YEAR

Similar to the black-capped chickadee but smaller, the 4½-inch Carolina has a shorter black bib, less white on its wings, and a shorter tail. Both sexes look alike.

VOICE: The *chick-a-dee-dee-dee* call is faster and higher-pitched than that of the black-capped, and the *phee-bee* song is four notes instead of two.

BEHAVIOR: The Carolina chickadee keeps to woodland areas and is attached to its southeastern home range.

HABITAT: The rural woodlands and coniferous forests of the Southeast, from coastal lowlands up to 4,000 feet.

NATURAL FOOD: Insects and their eggs and larvae; also seeds and fruits gleaned from southeastern woodlands.

NEST: A 5- to 6-inch hole about 5 or 6 feet above the ground is excavated by the nesting pair in soft or rotted wood over a 2-week period. They may also use an abandoned woodpecker hole or a birdhouse. Moss, animal hair, feathers, and plant down line the nest. The female incubates the 6 white eggs, spotted brown, for 13 days while the male brings her food. Young fly in about 2 weeks.

TO ATTRACT: Offer sunflower seeds, suet, and peanut butter mix, and erect a birdhouse (4 by 4 by 10 inches high with a 1¼-inch entrance hole) 5 feet high. Evergreens are appreciated for cover.

The 6-inch tufted titmouse is a mouselike bird with a gray crest, buff-colored flanks, and beady black eyes. Male and female look alike. In the West, this species is replaced by oak and juniper titmice.

VOICE: The familiar *pet-tow, pet-tow, pet-tow* brightens any woodland. The *day-day-day* alarm note sounds harsher and more demanding.

BEHAVIOR: The species has extended its range into the Northeast and upper Midwest and is usually in the company of chickadees and nuthatches as it forages noisily through woodlands.

HABITAT: Backyards and gardens; also forests, swamps, and orchards of the East.

NATURAL FOOD: Insects, their eggs, and larvae; seeds and fruits found in the woods. With its sharp, black bill, the tufted titmouse opens moth cocoons for the larvae inside.

NEST: The tufted titmouse nests in a tree cavity, often taking over a woodpecker hole. The 5 or 6 speckled and creamy eggs are incubated for 13 or 14 days by the female; the male calls her out to feed her. Young leave the nest 17 or 18 days after hatching.

TO ATTRACT: Titmice are fond of sunflower seeds and relish suet on cold days. Occasionally they'll use a birdhouse (4 by 4 by 10 inches high with a 1¼-inch entrance hole) placed 6 to 15 feet high. Oak trees may attract them.

TUFTED TITMOUSE
Baeolophus bicolor
CHICKADEE AND TITMOUSE FAMILY
(PARIDAE)

　　WINTER
　　BREEDING
　　ALL YEAR

A tiny, dull gray bird with brown cap or cheeks (varying regionally), long tail, and very short bill, the 3½-inch bushtit looks the same in either sex except for the eyes—dark brown for males (and young birds), cream-colored for females. Males of a southwestern variation have black eye patches.

VOICE: Bushtits are constantly vocal to keep their flock together, uttering *tsit-tsit-tsit* as they feed. They have no song.

BEHAVIOR: Bushtits are even more active than chickadees and titmice. Except during the breeding season, they're found in flocks numbering as few as 6 or as many as 50, foraging through thickets with other small birds.

HABITAT: Forest thickets, oak woodlands, chaparral, canyons, and streamsides.

NATURAL FOOD: Insects, insect eggs, and larvae; also fruits and seeds.

NEST: Male and female work together to weave a 6- to 8-inch gourd-shaped basket nest. The nest is built 6 to 35 feet high in a bush or tree and lined with moss, lichen, leaves, and spider silk. Both parents spend nights in the nest while incubating the 5 to 7 white eggs for 12 or 13 days. Young fly in about 2 weeks.

TO ATTRACT: Bushtits may come for sunflower seeds and suet but are most apt to appear near ponds and thick evergreen shrubs in sunny areas.

BUSHTIT
Psaltriparus minimus
BUSHTIT FAMILY (AEGITHALIDAE)

　　WINTER
　　BREEDING
　　ALL YEAR

RED-BREASTED NUTHATCH

Sitta canadensis
NUTHATCH FAMILY (SITTIDAE)

WINTER
BREEDING
ALL YEAR

The stubby little red-breasted nuthatch is a 4½-inch acrobat with a gray back, rusty breast, black cap, white eye line, and short tail. The female is a bit lighter in color. Like other nuthatches, this one hops down the tree head first.

VOICE: The song is a trumpetlike *wea-wea-wea-wea.* The alarm call is a more disturbed *tank-tank-tank-tank.*

BEHAVIOR: This species of the northern woods country may move south in great numbers in winter, when its natural foods are scarce. At the entrance to its nesting cavity in a dead or rotted tree, the bird dabs pine resin or pitch to discourage predators from entering. Sometimes it gets stuck, too.

HABITAT: Northern coniferous forests, but in winter also backyards and gardens.

NATURAL FOOD: The seeds of pines, firs, and spruces, mixed with insects, insect eggs, and larvae.

NEST: The nest is built 4 inches into an excavated tree cavity—sometimes a woodpecker hole—and lined with mosses, grasses, and feathers to protect the 5 or 6 reddish-spotted white eggs. The female incubates the eggs for 12 days; young fly about 3 weeks after hatching.

TO ATTRACT: Sunflower seeds, peanut kernels, and suet are favorite foods. Conifers will also attract the birds (they rarely use birdhouses).

WHITE-BREASTED NUTHATCH

Sitta carolinensis
NUTHATCH FAMILY (SITTIDAE)

WINTER
BREEDING
ALL YEAR

A 6-inch blue-gray bird with white breast and belly, black cap (gray for females in some regions), and stubby tail, the white-breasted nuthatch moves head first down tree trunks. The white-breasted wedges tree nuts and seeds into crevices in the tree bark to hammer them open with its bill; as a result, this bird was first called "nut-hack."

VOICE: The song is a series of rapid whistles—*whit-whi-whit-whi-whi.* The alarm note is a harsh *yank, yank, yank,* slower and more nasal than that of the red-breasted.

BEHAVIOR: White-breasted nuthatches often forage in the woods in the company of chickadees, titmice, and brown creepers. These "upside-down birds" can see food in bark crevices that birds coming up the trunk might miss.

HABITAT: Oaks and mixed woodlands, orchards, and mature trees in suburbs and cities.

NATURAL FOOD: Nuts and seeds in fall and winter, also insects in spring and summer.

NEST: A pair nests in a tree cavity (often in a woodpecker hole) 15 to 50 feet above the ground. The female lines the nest with bark shreds, twigs, grass, fur, and hair. Then she lays 8 white eggs, heavily marked with light brown spots, and incubates them for 12 days. Youngsters can fly in 2 weeks.

TO ATTRACT: One of the most common of all backyard species in the East and Midwest, the white-breasted nuthatch relishes sunflower seeds, peanut kernels, and suet.

BROWN CREEPER
Certhia americana
CREEPER FAMILY (CERTHIIDAE)

WINTER
BREEDING
ALL YEAR

Nearly invisible against tree bark, the 5-inch brown creeper is streaked brown above and white below, male and female alike. It has a sharp, slightly curved bill and a long, stiff tail which it uses to prop itself against tree trunks.

VOICE: The single high-pitched *seee* is hardly noticeable. In spring, the male sings a high-pitched *see-see-see-sisi-see.*

BEHAVIOR: Starting at the base of a tree, the brown creeper searches for food by working its way up in a spiraling path around the trunk until it reaches the top. Then it flies down to the base of a nearby tree and begins a new upward spiral.

HABITAT: Coniferous and deciduous forests, mixed woodlands and swamps, and wooded backyards throughout the continent.

NATURAL FOOD: Almost entirely insects gleaned from crevices in tree trunks.

NEST: The brown creeper hides its nest behind a loose slab of bark 5 to 15 feet or so above the ground. The nest is made by the female (assisted by her mate) out of leaves, twigs, and bark shreds, lined with finer bark shreds, grass, and moss. Both sexes incubate the 5 or 6 peppered white eggs for 14 or 15 days. Young spend 15 days in the nest.

TO ATTRACT: Though these birds seem to like suet, what they really like are the tiny insects that the suet attracts. They'll also come to conifers and big dead trees.

CAROLINA WREN
Thryothorus ludovicianus
WREN FAMILY (TROGLODYTIDAE)

WINTER
BREEDING
ALL YEAR

The East's largest wren, the 5½-inch Carolina is rich brown above a buff belly, with a white throat, tawny sides, and a conspicuous white eye line in both the male and the female.

VOICE: The Carolina's hearty *tea-kettle, tea-kettle, tea-kettle* is one of the definitive sounds of the South. Its alarm note is a buzzing noise that sounds like a thumb being rubbed against the teeth of a comb.

BEHAVIOR: Though its conspicuous song is bold, the Carolina is retiring, hiding in the deep tangles and brush of southeastern woodlands. Pioneers of this species have tried, with limited success, to expand its range northward into New England and the upper Midwest.

HABITAT: Brushy thickets and hedges and the tangles of suburban gardens in the East.

NATURAL FOOD: Primarily insects and also snails, small frogs, lizards, berries and other fruits.

NEST: The Carolina is a cavity nester, selecting a woodpecker hole, stone wall, or hole in an outbuilding as a site for its bulky nest of leaves, twigs, and weed stalks. Feathers, grass, moss, and hair line the nest. The female incubates the 5 or 6 spotted pink eggs for 14 days, while the attentive male feeds her. Young are out of the nest and on the wing within 2 weeks.

TO ATTRACT: Offer suet cakes mixed with cornmeal, sunflower seeds, and other seeds. A birdbath also attracts these wrens, and they seek thickets where they can hide.

HOUSE WREN
Troglodytes aedon
WREN FAMILY (TROGLODYTIDAE)

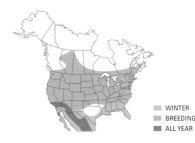

A little brown bird—that describes this plainest of all wrens. The 4½-inch house wren is dark brown above and light brown below, without any streaks or eye lines in either sex.

VOICE: The male's bubbling, chattering, repetitive song rises and then falls at the end. The species' scolding note is a series of *zzzzzzssszzz* sounds.

BEHAVIOR: The male arrives on the breeding grounds in spring a week or two before the female; he sings and builds dummy nests of sticks in several viable sites. When the female arrives, she either selects one of the nests or builds her own in a new location.

HABITAT: Backyards, farmlands, and open forests.

NATURAL FOOD: Nothing but insects, from caterpillars to grasshoppers to spiders.

NEST: Famous for where they nest—boots, car radiators, mailboxes, laundry on clotheslines—house wrens build stick nests lined with grass, plant fibers, feathers, and rubbish. In the wild, they choose a hole in a tree or other natural crevice. The 6 or 7 cinnamon-speckled white eggs are incubated by the female for about 13 days; young leave the nest in 12 to 18 days.

TO ATTRACT: House wrens are among the most common backyard nesters in North America; they can be lured with wren houses (4 by 4 by 6 inches high with a 1½-inch entrance hole) 6 to 10 feet above the ground. Try several in the same half-acre. Wrens also use brush, woodpiles, berry tangles, and wild areas.

GOLDEN-CROWNED KINGLET
Regulus satrapa
KINGLET FAMILY (REGULIDAE)

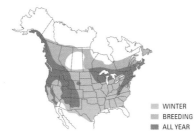

A tiny flit of a bird, the 3½-inch golden-crowned kinglet is olive green above and lighter below, with two white wing bars and a conspicuous crown of yellow and orange (male, pictured) or all yellow (female). Otherwise, male and female look the same.

VOICE: Unless your hearing is acute, you may miss this bird's call. The male's song is a high-pitched, descending *zee-zee-zee-zee;* the alarm note is a simple *tsee.*

BEHAVIOR: Ever flicking its wings, the little kinglet is constantly on the move, hopping from twig to twig and hovering as it feeds.

HABITAT: Coniferous forests, mainly spruces, but sometimes backyards and gardens with tall conifers during migrations.

NATURAL FOOD: Insects plucked from the needles and cones of spruces while the bird hovers in midair.

NEST: A hanging oblong mass of mosses and lichens is attached to the twigs of a horizontal spruce limb, some 6 to 60 feet high, then lined with fine bark, rootlets, and soft feathers. The 8 or 9 tiny eggs—cream blotched with brown—are laid in two layers in the nest and are believed to be incubated by the female alone for 14 or 15 days. Young can fly in 14 to 19 days.

TO ATTRACT: These birds don't eat birdseed, but they associate with species that do, including chickadees and brown creepers. They may come for suet in a wooded area.

The little ruby-crowned kinglet is an olive green birdlet with two white wing bars, one black wing bar, and a white eye ring. Male (pictured) and female of this 4-inch species are alike, except for the male's ruby red crown spot—usually hidden under olive green feathers.

VOICE: Its song is greatly out of proportion to this bird's size. Loud and husky notes start low and then rise high, *tee, tee, tue, tue, tue, ti-daddy, ti-daddy.* The *jee-didit* alarm note also seems loud.

BEHAVIOR: Ruby-crowneds always seem nervous, flitting their wings and hovering as they move through pine and spruce thickets, often in the company of warblers during migration.

HABITAT: Coniferous forests for breeding, but backyards during migration and western lowlands in winter.

NATURAL FOOD: Mostly insects caught by hovering in front of pine and spruce cones and needles; also some fruits and seeds.

NEST: The deep cup nest is well hidden beneath a horizontal spruce branch, 2 to 100 feet above the ground. Mosses, fur, and feathers line the nest. The female is completely concealed in the nest while she incubates 7 to 9 pale buff eggs dotted reddish brown for about 12 days. Young fly from the nest in another 12 days.

TO ATTRACT: Water attracts the birds during migration; suet appeals, too.

RUBY-CROWNED KINGLET
Regulus calendula
KINGLET FAMILY (REGULIDAE)

WINTER
BREEDING
ALL YEAR

Deep blue back, rusty red throat and breast, and white under the tail describes the male of the 7-inch eastern bluebird species (shown at right). The female's coloration is much duller (see below). Juveniles have spotted breasts.

VOICE: The male's melodious *chur-a-lee* song is a welcome sign of spring. Both sexes utter the shorter *chur-lee* call.

BEHAVIOR: Though these birds are solitary nesters, they're gregarious in the fall and winter, when they join forces to migrate and feed in flocks.

HABITAT: Open country on farms, along roadside fences, in open woodlands and swamps.

NATURAL FOOD: Insects and seeds. Eastern bluebirds flutter from fence posts and wires down to the ground when they spot food.

NEST: Unlike other thrushes, bluebirds often nest in woodpecker holes, natural tree cavities, or birdhouses. The carelessly arranged grass nest holds 4 or 5 pale bluish white eggs, incubated by the female for 13 to 15 days; young leave the nest 2 to 3 weeks later. Two broods per year are common.

TO ATTRACT: Eastern bluebirds will eat cornmeal mixed with suet and peanut butter; a better way to attract them is to put up birdhouses (5 by 5 by 8 inches high with a 1½-inch entrance hole) 5 to 10 feet high in an open field.

EASTERN BLUEBIRD
Sialia sialis
THRUSH FAMILY (TURDIDAE)

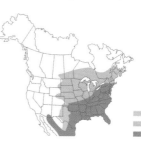

WINTER
BREEDING
ALL YEAR

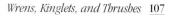

WESTERN BLUEBIRD

Sialia mexicana

THRUSH FAMILY (TURDIDAE)

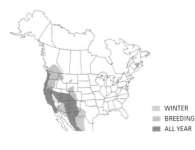

WINTER
BREEDING
ALL YEAR

Its blue back and throat, brick red breast, and gray undertail coverts identify the male western bluebird (right). Often the breast color extends across the shoulders and upper back of the 7-inch bird. The female (left) is duller overall. Juveniles have spotted breasts.

VOICE: The male's warbling *chu-a-wee* is harsher and shorter than the eastern bluebird's song. The *pew* call is uttered by both male and female.

BEHAVIOR: Western bluebirds must often compete with starlings and house sparrows for nesting sites, though they're compatible with pygmy nuthatches, northern flickers, tree swallows, and house wrens nesting in the same tree. In winter, bluebirds fly to lower elevations in flocks that rarely number more than 30—and often include a few yellow-rumped warblers.

HABITAT: Open farmlands, roadsides, and open woodlands in mountain regions.

NATURAL FOOD: Mostly insects; also berries and other fruits. The western bluebird can be seen darting out from a tree, post, or utility wire to catch insects on the wing.

NEST: Accompanied by the male, the female builds a grass nest, often in an old woodpecker hole, inside a tree cavity, or in a birdhouse. She lays 4 to 6 pale blue eggs and incubates them for 14 days.

TO ATTRACT: Fruit may attract these birds to feeders, but they're more apt to be interested in birdhouses (5 by 5 by 8 inches deep with a 1½-inch entrance hole) erected 5 to 10 feet high in open fields. Old fruit orchards appeal as nest sites, too.

MOUNTAIN BLUEBIRD

Sialia currucoides

THRUSH FAMILY (TURDIDAE)

WINTER
BREEDING
ALL YEAR

A true blue bird, the male 7-inch sky blue mountain bluebird is blue all over—light underneath, deeper above (see photo). The female is mostly gray, blue only on the wings. Young birds are dark gray with spotted breasts.

VOICE: The male's high-pitched warbling whistle, *tru-lee,* resembles that of the American robin. During migration and in winter flocks, birds utter a *veer* note.

BEHAVIOR: This bird lives at elevations up to 12,000 feet during the breeding season. Nests are often located among other species; at least one pair has been known to use a cliff swallow nest within a cliff swallow colony.

HABITAT: At high altitudes in open rangeland, mountain meadows, and open wooded parkland.

NATURAL FOOD: Insects, pursued by hovering over grasslands or darting out from rocks; also berries and other fruits.

NEST: Like other bluebirds, this one builds a grass nest in a natural cavity, often an old woodpecker hole; both sexes contribute to the chore. The female incubates her 5 or 6 very pale blue eggs for 14 days, and young fly in 3 weeks.

TO ATTRACT: Mountain bluebirds aren't likely to come to feeders, but they will nest in birdhouses (5 by 5 by 8 inches high with a 1½-inch entrance hole) 5 to 10 feet above the ground in an open meadow. They'll also nest in dead trees, and they like old orchards.

A plump bird with a rusty red back, the 8-inch wood thrush is brighter red about the head. Its white breast is marked with large round or oval black dots. Male and female look alike.

VOICE: The male's memorable flutelike song, *gerald-deeeen,* is a magical sound of the spring woods. Both sexes utter the alarm call, a rapid *pit, pit, pit.*

BEHAVIOR: Originally a bird of deep, damp forests, the wood thrush is apparently becoming more tolerant of humans, nesting more frequently in garden shrubbery.

HABITAT: Mostly on or near the ground in cool, wet forests or in eastern parks and backyards that offer similar conditions.

NATURAL FOOD: Insects, snails, and earthworms, as well as berries and other fruits. The wood thrush is a ground feeder.

NEST: The compact, cuplike nest is anchored about 10 feet above the ground in the crotch of a horizontal tree limb. Constructed by the female of grass, bark, moss, paper, and mud, it's molded to fit her body. She incubates her 3 or 4 bluish green eggs for 13 days; when she goes away, the male stands guard. Young fly in about 2 weeks.

TO ATTRACT: Wood thrushes may eat fruit at feeders or from berry-producing plants during the warm months. Large shrubs or small garden trees surrounded by dark woodlands may attract as nesting sites.

WOOD THRUSH
Hylocichla mustelina
THRUSH FAMILY (TURDIDAE)

■ WINTER
■ BREEDING
■ ALL YEAR

The familiar 10-inch American robin has a slate gray back and brick red breast. It also has a white eye ring, streaked white throat, and yellow bill. The male's head is a darker gray than its back (see photo); the female is paler overall. Juveniles have spotted breasts.

VOICE: The male carols a welcome c*heer-o-lee, cheer-o-lee, cheer-o-lee* song. Its *tut, tut, tut* alarm call is demanding.

BEHAVIOR: Males return to their northern breeding grounds before the females, establishing and defending territories vigorously. In warmer regions, American robins stay all year long.

HABITAT: Suburban and city lawns and gardens, parks, and open woodlands. In the West, robins may nest at altitudes up to 12,000 feet.

NATURAL FOOD: Largely earthworms (located by sight, not sound); also insects, berries, and other fruits.

NEST: Built in a fork or on a horizontal branch of a tree or shrub—or on a ledge, door light, or downspout—the deep cup nest of mud and grass is molded by the female's body. Four "robin's-egg blue" eggs are incubated by the female for 12 to 14 days, and the young leave the nest in about 2 weeks. Two broods annually are common, but rarely at the same site.

TO ATTRACT: During late spring snowstorms, robins may eat fruit, suet, or peanut butter mix placed on or near the ground. They relish berries and fruits borne on shrubs and trees.

AMERICAN ROBIN
Turdus migratorius
THRUSH FAMILY (TURDIDAE)

■ WINTER
■ BREEDING
■ ALL YEAR

GRAY CATBIRD
Dumetella carolinensis
MIMIC THRUSH FAMILY (MIMIDAE)

WINTER
BREEDING
ALL YEAR

A slim relative of the mockingbird, the 9-inch gray catbird is all gray except for a cap and long tail of black and rusty undertail coverts. Male and female look the same.

VOICE: Its catlike *mew* gave this bird its name. The male's song is a lively series of unrelated and often disjointed musical notes and phrases. In the evening, the male may sing a quiet whisper song. The *chuck* alarm call is a scolding sound.

BEHAVIOR: An unimpressive appearance is more than compensated for by many calls and songs. Besides their own distinctive calls, catbirds imitate other bird songs and even tree frog sounds, as well as some man-made noises.

HABITAT: Thickets, woodlands, undergrowth, hedges, and garden shrubbery.

NATURAL FOOD: Insects collected on or near the ground (more than half its diet); also berries and other fruits.

NEST: The bulky nest of twigs, vines, leaves, and paper is built by both parents and is well concealed in a dense thicket, thick shrubbery, or briers 3 to 10 feet above the ground. Deep and cuplike, it is lined with rootlets. The female lays 4 deep greenish blue eggs and incubates them for 12 or 13 days. The young fly in about 2 weeks.

TO ATTRACT: Catbirds may eat fruit at feeders, also from shrubs, trees, and vines. They enjoy bathing and drinking at birdbaths.

NORTHERN MOCKINGBIRD
Mimus polyglottos
MIMIC THRUSH FAMILY (MIMIDAE)

WINTER
BREEDING
ALL YEAR

White wing patches and white outer tail feathers, conspicuous in flight, are distinctive field marks of an otherwise dull gray bird. Male and female of the 10-inch northern mockingbird look alike.

VOICE: Named for its creative repertoire of songs and noises—one-third its own and two-thirds mimicry—the northern mockingbird is adept at imitating both avian and man-made sounds. Even ringing alarm clocks and factory whistles are copied. Its own alarm note is a harsh *tchack*.

BEHAVIOR: Males are famous for singing at night—particularly on warm nights, it seems, when people are trying to sleep with their windows open.

HABITAT: Hedges and thickets of backyards, farmlands, and brushy woodlands.

NATURAL FOOD: Animal matter (more than half the diet), mostly insects flushed when the bird raises its wings, angel-like; also berries and other fruits.

NEST: The bulky nest is hidden 3 to 10 feet above the ground in a thicket. The male suggests nesting sites by placing material, but the female has the final say. Both build. Four light blue-green eggs, heavily blotched with brown, are incubated by the female for 12 or 13 days. Youngsters vacate the nest 10 to 12 days after hatching.

TO ATTRACT: Offer suet mixed with cornmeal and grow native berry-producing plants. Thorny plants offer nest sites.

The fox-red back and heavily streaked whitish breast of the 11-inch brown thrasher are conspicuous as the long-tailed bird streaks across backyards. Upon closer inspection, a bright yellow eye (in young birds, the iris is light blue) and down-curved bill are also evident. Both sexes look alike.

VOICE: Like other members of the mockingbird tribe, the brown thrasher has a repertoire of sounds—some musical, some mechanical, most mimicked. Usually each phrase is repeated: *see it, see it; hello, hello; say what, say what.* The alarm note is a loud *smak.*

BEHAVIOR: The male usually gives his concert from the top of a tree or shrub, head held high and long tail down.

HABITAT: Thickets and hedges of suburban and city backyards and farmlands.

NATURAL FOOD: Insects seized by the bird's long, curved bill as it thrashes in dead leaves; salamanders, snakes, lizards; also berries and other fruits.

NEST: Brown thrashers hide their bulky nests of twigs, grasses, and vines anywhere from ground level to 14 feet high in thickets. Both parents incubate their 4 pale bluish white eggs (marked with fine reddish spots) for 12 or 13 days. Young leave the nest in about 2 weeks.

TO ATTRACT: Set out seeds and suet mixed with cornmeal. Low shrubs, brush piles, and berry-producing plants are also appealing.

BROWN THRASHER
Toxostoma rufum
MIMIC THRUSH FAMILY (MIMIDAE)

WINTER
BREEDING
ALL YEAR

Introduced more than a century ago in New York City, the 8-inch European starling has spread through most of North America. In spring and summer, it is iridescent black, green, and purple with a bright yellow bill (shown at left); it turns speckled, with a greenish bill, in fall and winter (photo below). Male and female look alike.

VOICE: A drawn-out whistle is its best-known sound, but the starling utters a variety of squawks and chatters and will also imitate other birds.

EUROPEAN STARLING
Sturnus vulgaris
STARLING FAMILY (STURNIDAE)

WINTER
BREEDING
ALL YEAR

BEHAVIOR: This starling has displaced many native birds from nesting cavities; populations of eastern bluebirds, woodpeckers, great-crested and ash-throated flycatchers have decreased as a result. In giant flocks, starlings can cause extensive crop damage, though their consumption of insect pests on farms can be beneficial.

HABITAT: Most often cities and suburbs, but also farmlands, wooded lots, and parks.

NATURAL FOOD: Insects, snails, earthworms; garbage; grain, weed seeds, berries, and other fruits.

NEST: Starlings nest 10 to 25 feet high in woodpecker holes, birdhouses, or any nook or cranny. Their messy collection of nesting materials ranges from grasses and twigs to feathers and trash. Both parents incubate 4 or 5 pale bluish green eggs for about 12 days. Young leave the nest in about 3 weeks and are on their own a few days later.

TO ATTRACT: Most people don't try to attract starlings, but they'll come to feeders.

CEDAR WAXWING
Bombycilla cedrorum
WAXWING FAMILY (BOMBYCILLIDAE)

WINTER
BREEDING
ALL YEAR

An elegant 7-inch bird of silky brown and tan with inner wing tips resembling dabs of red sealing wax, the cedar waxwing also has a yellow tip on its tail, a yellow belly, and a black mask. The two sexes look alike.

VOICE: The wheezing call is high pitched and often difficult to hear.

BEHAVIOR: If you see one cedar waxwing, you almost always see a small flock. These gregarious birds stay together throughout the year, nesting in loose colonies.

HABITAT: Open groves, orchards, urban and suburban back-yards, and wild areas where native berries grow.

NATURAL FOOD: Insects and berries, including berries of cedar and mountain ash trees. Cedar waxwings are known for fluttering out from trees to capture insects and for gorging on berries.

NEST: These late nesters build their loosely woven nest of grass, twigs, and sometimes yarn on a horizontal branch 4 to 50 feet above the ground. Both sexes work on the nest for 5 to 7 days, finishing it with a lining of rootlets, fine grasses, and plant down. The 4 or 5 pale gray eggs, blotched dark brown, are incubated by the female for 12 or 13 days. Young leave 2 to 2½ weeks after hatching.

TO ATTRACT: Water attracts for drinking and bathing. You can also grow native berry-producing plants as a lure.

YELLOW WARBLER
Dendroica petechia
WARBLER FAMILY (PARULIDAE)

WINTER
BREEDING
ALL YEAR

The male yellow warbler is a 5-inch, bright yellow bird with olive yellow back and red breast streaks (see photo). The female is similar but duller, without streaking.

VOICE: The male's cheerful song is a series of *sweet, sweet, sweet* notes ending with *I'm so sweet.* The call or alarm note is a simple *chip.*

BEHAVIOR: The yellow warbler is a common victim of the brown-headed cowbird, which tosses the warbler eggs out of the nest and replaces them with its own, but the warbler simply builds more nest on top to cover the cowbird eggs. As many as six stories of nest have been found covering cowbird eggs.

HABITAT: Hedges, roadside thickets, stream banks, and garden shrubbery.

NATURAL FOOD: Insects—including many destructive ones—and their larvae.

NEST: By itself or in a loose colony, the yellow warbler builds its nest 3 to 8 feet above the ground in the upright fork of a shrub or brier. The female completes the nest in about 4 days using plant down, hair, and grasses, lays 4 or 5 bluish white eggs with brown markings, and incubates them for 11 or 12 days. Young fly in 9 to 12 days.

TO ATTRACT: Running water will attract yellow warblers, especially near willows; multiflora roses and other thick shrubbery appeal as nesting sites. In the West, where deciduous forests are uncommon, these birds depend greatly on mature streamside woods.

Once considered two species—the western Audubon's and more easterly Myrtle's warblers—this 5½-inch bird displays a bright yellow rump, yellow side patches, and a white belly and undertail. Warblers of the Audubon's type have a yellow throat oval; Myrtle's birds (male shown in photo) have a white throat extending narrowly onto the sides of the neck. In breeding plumage, all males are blue-black above with variable amounts of black on the breast; by fall, the black fades to a dull olive brown. Females are paler and less marked than breeding males.

VOICE: The song is a trilled soft whistle, variable toward the end. The call is a fairly loud *chip*, somewhat higher in Audubon's than in Myrtle's.

BEHAVIOR: Yellow-rumps form winter feeding flocks with other insectivore species. These flocks sometimes number in the hundreds. The birds forage from the ground to the treetops and often take insects on the wing.

HABITAT: Coniferous and mixed forests for nesting; parks, urban and suburban gardens, and temperate forests in winter.

NATURAL FOOD: Mostly insects and spiders, also berries.

NEST: Mid-level to high on a horizontal conifer branch, the female builds a cup made of hair, bark, grass, twigs, or other plant fiber, usually lined with feathers. She incubates 3 to 5 off-white, speckled brown eggs for 12 or 13 days; both parents feed the young, which fledge at 13 or 14 days.

TO ATTRACT: Mature conifers attract as nest sites. In winter, provide water, berry-producing plants, winter-flowering eucalyptus, and suet. Yellow-rumps have occasionally been recorded at seed feeders.

YELLOW-RUMPED WARBLER
Dendroica coronata
WARBLER FAMILY (PARULIDAE)

WINTER
BREEDING
ALL YEAR

The 7-inch brilliant red scarlet tanager male has glossy black wings and tail and no crest. Females (shown below right) and immature birds—and males in winter—have dull green backs, yellow bellies, and blackish wings and tails.

VOICE: Like an American robin with a sore throat, the male sings a series of 4 or 5 hoarse, caroling notes: *queer-it, queer, queer-it, queer*. Its call is *chip-churr.*

BEHAVIOR: Males arrive at their breeding territory several days before the females. They sing from the tallest trees to attract females and defend their turf.

HABITAT: Thick groves of deciduous trees and conifers, parks, suburban backyards.

NATURAL FOOD: Insects, berries and other fruits, and seeds. Scarlet tanagers forage both in the trees where they sing and nest and on the ground beneath.

NEST: Well out on a limb, 8 to 75 feet above ground, the female builds a flat nest cup of twigs and rootlets lined with fine grasses. She then lays 3 to 5 pale blue or green eggs spotted with brown. She alone incubates the eggs, for 13 or 14 days, but both parents feed the young during the 2 weeks they're in the nest.

TO ATTRACT: Tall deciduous trees help to attract. Tanagers will eat cornmeal mixed with peanut butter and suet and will bathe in and drink from backyard ponds.

SCARLET TANAGER
Piranga olivacea
TANAGER FAMILY (THRAUPIDAE)

WINTER
BREEDING
ALL YEAR

WESTERN TANAGER
Piranga ludoviciana
TANAGER FAMILY (THRAUPIDAE)

WINTER
BREEDING
ALL YEAR

With its beautiful red head and face, yellow body, and black wings marked with two prominent white or yellowish bars, the 7-inch male western tanager is an eye-catching bird (photo at right). In winter, like females all year, males are dull olive green above and yellow below, with wing bars.

VOICE: The male's hoarse, robinlike song is sung in 2 or 3 liquid phrases. Its call or alarm is *pit-trick.*

BEHAVIOR: These birds of the high West spend much of their time in the tops of trees, often on the same perches for long periods of time. Though the birds blend into their habitat, making them difficult to see, you can locate males by searching in the direction of their songs.

HABITAT: Coniferous and pine-oak forests.

NATURAL FOOD: Mostly insects, but also berries and other fruits.

NEST: The flat, loosely built cup of coniferous twigs and rootlets is usually saddled 20 to 30 feet high in the fork of a horizontal branch in a pine, fir, oak, or aspen tree and lined with hair and rootlets. The 3 to 5 spotted bluish green eggs are incubated by the female for 13 days. Both parents feed the young.

TO ATTRACT: Offer citrus fruits and juices, also hummingbird feeders. Migrating birds feed in western flowering eucalyptus; they may nest in tall pines in gardens.

SPOTTED AND EASTERN TOWHEE
Pipilo maculatus,
Pipilo erythrophthalmus
TOWHEE AND SPARROW FAMILY
(EMBERIZIDAE)

Spotted towhee   Eastern towhee

WINTER   BREEDING   ALL YEAR

Slightly smaller (7½ inches) and more slender than an American robin, spotted and eastern towhee males are mostly black with a white belly and rufous flanks. The spotted also has white spots on its back and wings. Female spotted towhees are a shade duller than the males. Eastern females are brown where the males are black.

VOICE: The familiar spring song of the eastern towhee is *drink your teeeee;* its call is a plaintive *toe-whee.* The spotted towhee sings a trill that's sometimes preceded by introductory notes; its call is a catlike *guee.*

BEHAVIOR: Towhees can be heard thrashing around in dead leaves under shrubs, searching for food, or singing from the tops of low shrubs.

HABITAT: Eastern towhees frequent thickets, hedgerows, fencerows, and brushy woodlands. Spotted towhees prefer chaparral, mountain manzanita thickets, scrub oaks, and the dense understory of piñon-juniper woods. Both visit garden shrubbery.

NATURAL FOOD: Mostly insects, spiders, snails, and other organisms found under the dead leaves in a thicket; also berries and other fruits found on or near the ground.

NEST: The female builds a bulky leaf and twig nest, on or near the ground; she then lays 3 to 5 cream-colored eggs with reddish spots and incubates them for 12 or 13 days. Young fledge in 10 to 12 days.

TO ATTRACT: Place birdseed and beef suet in tray feeders. Ponds also attract.

Spotted towhee male

Eastern towhee female

The little sparrow with a brick red cap is probably a chipping sparrow if you see it hopping around in summer, but it's likely to be the 6-inch American tree sparrow if you spot it in winter within its range. Male and female look alike, marked with a black dot in the center of the breast (unlike the chipping sparrow, below) and a bill that's dark above and light below.

VOICE: Males tune up their cheerful, trilling song in spring before heading off to breeding grounds in the far North. Otherwise, they utter a simple *teesip*.

BEHAVIOR: Misnamed "tree" sparrow because it looks like the tree sparrow of Europe, the American tree sparrow actually spends most of its time on the ground.

HABITAT: In winter, the species migrates south to the United States and southern Canada, where it lives in brushy fields, in fencerows, and around backyard feeders.

NATURAL FOOD: In winter, the seeds of weeds, grasses, and crops; in summer, also insects and berries.

NEST: The female builds a nest of grass and moss on or near the ground, then lays 3 to 5 pale greenish white eggs speckled brown. She incubates them for 12 or 13 days; young leave the nest in about 10 days, before they can fly.

TO ATTRACT: Offer birdseed mixtures with red and white millet. This sparrow likes weedy garden edges and seeds of annuals and perennials.

If there's a 5-inch sparrow with brick red cap, warm brown back, and light underside feeding on the ground in your garden, it's very likely a chipping sparrow. Check for a white line above a black line running through the eye. Juveniles have streaky brown caps and striped underparts (in winter all birds resemble immature birds without the breast streaking). Male and female look alike.

VOICE: Its song is an insectlike trill, and its alarm call is a simple *tsip*.

BEHAVIOR: This common ground sparrow is tame, quiet, and at home even at the back door.

HABITAT: On the ground in and around towns, villages, farms, and pine plantations.

NATURAL FOOD: Mostly grass and weed seeds; also many insects during summer.

NEST: The female builds a nest of fine grasses and weed stalks 3 to 10 feet above the ground, usually in a small conifer; she lines it with fine grasses and hair, sometimes human hair. Four bluish green eggs with dark blotches are incubated by the female for 11 to 14 days while her mate feeds her on the nest. The young fly at about 1½ weeks.

TO ATTRACT: Offer red and white millet, cracked corn, and water. Weedy garden edges and small seeds of annuals and perennials appeal.

AMERICAN TREE SPARROW
Spizella arborea
TOWHEE AND SPARROW FAMILY
(EMBERIZIDAE)

WINTER
BREEDING
ALL YEAR

CHIPPING SPARROW
Spizella passerina
TOWHEE AND SPARROW FAMILY
(EMBERIZIDAE)

WINTER
BREEDING
ALL YEAR

SONG SPARROW

MeloSpiza melodia

TOWHEE AND SPARROW FAMILY
(EMBERIZIDAE)

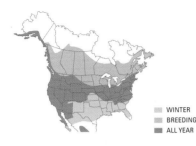

WINTER
BREEDING
ALL YEAR

The most widespread of all North American sparrows, this 6-inch bird has a brown back and a heavily streaked breast with a large central breast spot. Male and female look the same. The 30 or so recognized subspecies vary in coloration.

VOICE: A welcome sound on the first warm day of spring, the song begins with two ringing notes, *sweet, sweet,* and then launches into a jumble of tones. The call or alarm note is a loud *chimp.*

BEHAVIOR: Tail dipping is common, but behavior and voice vary in subspecies.

HABITAT: On or near the ground where there's abundant natural cover, on farms, and in cities and suburbs.

NATURAL FOOD: Insect matter foraged from the ground; also a variety of seeds, berries, and other fruits.

NEST: The well-hidden ground nest is built by the female in 5 to 10 days, using grasses, weed stems, leaves, and a lining of fine grasses, rootlets, and hair. The 3 to 5 greenish white eggs, heavily dotted reddish brown, are incubated by the female for 12 or 13 days. Young are out of the nest, often before they can fly, in about 10 days.

TO ATTRACT: Provide birdseed at ground feeders and water. Thickets, brush piles, and tangles (especially moist berry-producing plants) are also attractions.

WHITE-THROATED SPARROW

Zonotrichia albicollis

TOWHEE AND SPARROW FAMILY
(EMBERIZIDAE)

WINTER
BREEDING
ALL YEAR

The 6-inch white-throated sparrow does have a white throat, but it also has a black-and-white striped crown, a yellow patch in front of each eye, a streaked brown back, and a gray breast. Male and female look the same. Immature birds have tan-and-brown striped crowns.

VOICE: The familiar song—*old sam peabody, peabody, peabody*—can be heard from late winter into spring. The call note is a forceful *chink.*

BEHAVIOR: A scratcher, the gregarious white-throated sparrow is usually found or heard in thickets as it scratches up snow or dead leaves in search of food.

HABITAT: Undergrowth and edges of fields and forests; backyards during migration.

NATURAL FOOD: Weed seeds and the fruits of trees and shrubs foraged from the ground in thickets; insects and other animal matter when available.

NEST: On or close to the ground under a brush pile or fallen tree, the female builds a grass nest and lines it with pine needles and bark fibers for her 3 to 5 cream-colored eggs, densely dotted with brown. She incubates the eggs 12 to 14 days. Young leave the nest at about 10 days and learn to fly a few days later.

TO ATTRACT: In the East, offer red and white millet and cracked corn on or near the ground to attract the birds during migrations.

The rather large (6½-inch) white-crowned sparrow has a high, puffy black-and-white striped crown, pale throat, gray breast, and brown streaked back. Its pink or yellow bill is another identifying mark. Both sexes look alike; young birds have tan-and-brown striped crowns.

VOICE: The first two notes of the song are sad whistles, followed by a jumbled trill. The call or alarm is a smart *seet*.

BEHAVIOR: In winter, when the birds are most often seen, they live in flocks of 6 to 15 in the East and as many as 200 in the West. Some subspecies nest in U.S. mountain ranges and along the West Coast.

WINTER
BREEDING
ALL YEAR

HABITAT: Alpine meadows, forest edges and clearings, brushy burns, chaparral, weedy fields, and backyards.

NATURAL FOOD: Seeds, sprouts, and other plant material; also insects. This bird can be found scratching vigorously for food under leaves or snow.

NEST: Set into a matting of dense vegetation on or near the ground, the nest is built by the female of fine twigs, grasses, and feathers and then lined with hair and feathers. The female incubates the 4 or 5 eggs, pale greenish with numerous reddish spots, for about 12 days. Young are out in another 10 days.

TO ATTRACT: During migrations, these birds will stop for birdseed on or near the ground. They relish weed seeds in any habitat.

Sometimes called "snowbird," the 6-inch dark-eyed junco is slate gray with a white belly and white outer tail feathers. The western "Oregon junco" form of the species (shown below right) has a dark head and brown back and wings. Male and female are similar, but immature birds are lighter in color.

VOICE: The musical spring song is a monotonous trill. The winter *tic* call is heard often.

WINTER
BREEDING
ALL YEAR

BEHAVIOR: Dark-eyed juncos forage for seeds on the ground in open areas. They're gregarious in winter, usually living in loose-knit flocks.

HABITAT: Thickets and edges of coniferous woodlands, mixed forests, and in winter, backyards and gardens across the continent.

NATURAL FOOD: Seeds, buds, and sprouts; in summer, insects found in coniferous forests.

NEST: Under an overhang of tree roots, a fallen tree, or a road embankment, the junco conceals its nest of grasses, rootlets, and mosses lined with finer plant materials and hair. The male helps carry materials for the female builder; she incubates her 4 or 5 pale gray eggs, marked with heavy reddish dots, for 12 or 13 days. Young leave in about 2 weeks.

TO ATTRACT: Offer red and white millet, cracked corn, and other small grains on or near the ground. Conifers attract, as do weedy edges and annual and perennial seeds.

NORTHERN CARDINAL
Cardinalis cardinalis
CARDINAL FAMILY (CARDINALIDAE)

WINTER
BREEDING
ALL YEAR

The spectacular 8-inch male northern cardinal is brilliant red with a patch of black at the base of his conical red bill and a prominent crest that he can raise or lower for effect. The attractive female (left in photo) is the same shape but in yellow tan plumage accented with red wings, crest, tail, and bill.

VOICE: The male's *what-cheer, what-cheer, birdie, birdie, birdie* song is a welcome sound at any time of the year. The female may call the same notes, but more softly. Their forceful alarm call is a harsh *chip*.

BEHAVIOR: Northern cardinals use their heavy, sharp bills to crack seeds.

HABITAT: Thickets, forest edges, suburban hedges, and garden shrubbery.

NATURAL FOOD: Seeds in winter; a variety of beetles, cicadas, and other insects during warm months; the fruits of trees, shrubs, and vines when available.

NEST: The bulky nest of twigs, vines, and leaves is hidden in a deep thicket, generally no higher than 10 feet above ground. The female lines the nest with fine grasses and hair, sometimes assisted by the male. The 3 or 4 bluish or greenish white eggs blotched with brown are incubated by the female, and occasionally by the male, for 12 or 13 days. Young fly about 12 days after hatching.

TO ATTRACT: Northern cardinals are fond of sunflower seeds, cracked corn, and safflower seeds. They'll also bathe and drink from garden ponds.

ROSE-BREASTED GROSBEAK
Pheucticus ludovicianus
CARDINAL FAMILY (CARDINALIDAE)

WINTER
BREEDING
ALL YEAR

A heavy, conical bill and the male's rosy red bib give the 8-inch rose-breasted grosbeak its name. The male (right) is strikingly patterned in black and white with a heart-shaped red bib and a cream-colored bill. His flashy flight pattern is highlighted by pink underwing linings. The female (left) is considerably duller, with brown and white stripes and a white line above the eye.

VOICE: The male's song resembles that of the American robin, but richer and more melodious. The alarm note is a loud *chink*.

BEHAVIOR: These quiet birds of summer sing beautifully, appear to be devoted mates, and visit feeders throughout the breeding season.

HABITAT: Mature deciduous woodlands, swamp borders, and orchards; also backyards and gardens surrounded by mature woods.

NATURAL FOOD: Blossoms, seeds, and insects in deciduous treetops.

NEST: The flimsy nest of sticks, 10 to 15 feet high in the fork of a deciduous tree or shrub, isn't dense enough to mask the 4 pale green, brown-blotched eggs from view below. Both parents incubate for 12 to 14 days, often singing. Young fly in about 15 days.

TO ATTRACT: Plant shrubs and trees that produce flowers and berries or other fruits. Offer sunflower seeds and a birdbath.

Patterned in rich orange and black, the 7-inch black-headed grosbeak male (pictured) has black-and-white wings, a black head, and a conical bill. The female is a warm brown with black-and-white head stripes.

VOICE: The song is a rich version of the American robin's, with more trilling notes and more abrupt phrases.

BEHAVIOR: Males arrive at their breeding grounds a week before females. When the females arrive, males begin their courtship, singing during hovering flight (otherwise, most singing is from a high perch).

HABITAT: Second-growth deciduous and coniferous forests, willow and cottonwood thickets, orchards, and western backyards and gardens where mature woodland prevails.

NATURAL FOOD: Seeds and buds of pines and other trees, wild fruits, and berries; insects found in the trees where the birds live.

NEST: Four to 12 feet high in the fork of a small tree, the female builds a bulky nest of twigs, rootlets, and grass stems. The 3 or 4 pale green eggs, dotted brown, are incubated for 12 or 13 days by both parents. Young birds are out of the nest about 12 days after hatching.

TO ATTRACT: Besides relishing sunflower and other seeds, black-headed grosbeaks are fond of a variety of coniferous and deciduous trees and shrubs.

Under some light conditions, the plumage of the 5½-inch male indigo bunting looks black, but its usual appearance is deep indigo blue. The female looks so different in her plain brown plumage that she doesn't even seem to be the same species.

VOICE: The male's song of summer is a lazily unfolding rhythm—*sweet, sweet; zee, zee; seer, seer; sip, sip.* The alarm note is a simple *sick.*

BEHAVIOR: The male arrives on the breeding grounds in spring and defends its territory vigorously by singing late into summer after most birds have stopped.

HABITAT: Borders, woodland edges, and brushy clearings with lush undergrowth.

NATURAL FOOD: Insects, berries, and seeds.

NEST: The crotch of a shrub or small tree, 2 to 12 feet high, is usually where the female carefully weaves a nest of grasses, bark strips, and weeds and then lines it with fine grasses and rootlets. She incubates the 3 or 4 pale bluish white eggs for 12 or 13 days. In another 10 days the young leave the nest.

TO ATTRACT: These avid seed-eaters will come for thistle (Niger seed), cracked sunflower seed, or millet during the summer breeding season, and they love birdbaths. Weedy edges of wooded gardens and annual and perennial seeds also attract.

BLACK-HEADED GROSBEAK
Pheucticus melanocephalus
CARDINAL FAMILY (CARDINALIDAE)

WINTER
BREEDING
ALL YEAR

INDIGO BUNTING
Passerina cyanea
CARDINAL FAMILY (CARDINALIDAE)

WINTER
BREEDING
ALL YEAR

PAINTED BUNTING
Passerina ciris
CARDINAL FAMILY (CARDINALIDAE)

■ WINTER
■ BREEDING
■ ALL YEAR

Among the most beautifully colored of all birds, the male painted bunting has a violet blue head, red underparts and rump, and a green back. The female of this 5½-inch species is very plain green above and lemon below.

VOICE: From a high, visible perch, the male sings its bright and pleasant warbling song. The alarm note is a single sharp *chip.*

BEHAVIOR: Despite his gaudy appearance, the male blends in amazingly well in the lush vegetation in which he lives. He defends his territory with surprising aggression for a bird his size.

HABITAT: Brushy fields, roadside hedges, fencerows, and thickets in southern backyards and gardens.

NATURAL FOOD: Seeds and insects foraged from the ground.

NEST: The female attaches her shallow nest cup to supporting vegetation 3 to 6 feet above the ground in a small tree or shrub. She incubates the 3 or 4 pale white eggs, spotted reddish brown, for 11 or 12 days. When young leave the nest after 2 weeks, the female continues to feed them while gathering nesting material for her next brood. Painted buntings sometimes have as many as 4 broods in a single nesting season.

TO ATTRACT: Though many painted buntings leave the country in winter, many others remain as faithful visitors to gardens offering seeds and pools.

RED-WINGED BLACKBIRD
Agelaius phoeniceus
BLACKBIRD FAMILY (ICTERIDAE)

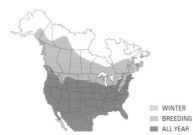

■ WINTER
■ BREEDING
■ ALL YEAR

This 9-inch black bird with a red-and-yellow chevron on each wing is one of the most widespread and best-known birds on the continent. Females and young birds are quite different in their sparrowlike brown-striped plumage.

VOICE: The male's *kong-ga-ree* song heralds spring from still-frozen marshes across the North. The birds' *chink* call or alarm note sounds quite demanding.

BEHAVIOR: Males arrive at their breeding grounds before the females, set up territories, and defend them vigorously against other males. If there's a surplus of females, males may be polygamous.

HABITAT: Fresh and saltwater marshes; swamps; wet meadows, pastures, and ditches.

NATURAL FOOD: About three-fourths vegetable matter (cultivated grains, weed seeds, and fruits); the remainder animal matter (insects, spiders, mollusks, snails).

NEST: In loose colonies, females build nests amid cattails, reeds, grasses, cultivated crops, and shrubs, usually near water. Nests are constructed of grasses, sedge leaves, and rushes bound to living vegetation and lined with fine grasses. The 3 or 4 pale blue eggs, scrawled in brown and purple, are incubated by the female for 10 to 12 days. Young climb out in about 10 days and then learn to fly.

TO ATTRACT: Cracked corn in any kind of feeder, but preferably a tray, will attract these birds, even while they're nesting nearby.

Though separate species, these two meadowlarks are virtually identical in appearance (a western is shown below; an eastern, at right). Chunky 10-inch birds with short tails, long bills, and buff brown backs, both are distinguished by a dramatic black V falling from the throat onto the yellow breast. Male and female are equally colorful.

VOICE: Only by their songs can one easily differentiate between the two meadowlarks. The western's song is melodious, with a flutelike babbling and gurgling; the eastern's is a more homogeneous, plaintive whistling. The western's call is a sharp *chuck;* the eastern's, a buzzing *dzrrt.*

BEHAVIOR: Males sing from fence posts or utility wires within their nesting territories; they may be polygamous. Females are very secretive.

HABITAT: Open grassy fields, meadows, prairies.

NATURAL FOOD: Insects (three-fourths of the diet) and grains. The birds forage by walking, not hopping.

NEST: The nest is built in a ground depression in a grassy field by the female in about a week, using dried grass and topping the structure with a domed roof. She incubates the 3 to 5 spotted white eggs for 13 to 15 days; both sexes bring food to the young, who leave the nest in about 2 weeks.

TO ATTRACT: Backyards with prairielike conditions—large, unmowed lawns and fields of short grass—may attract meadowlarks searching for nesting sites and grain.

WESTERN AND EASTERN MEADOWLARK
Sturnella neglecta, Sturnella magna
BLACKBIRD FAMILY (ICTERIDAE)

Western meadowlark | Eastern meadowlark

WINTER | BREEDING | ALL YEAR

COMMON GRACKLE
Quiscalus quiscula
BLACKBIRD FAMILY (ICTERIDAE)

WINTER
BREEDING
ALL YEAR

A 12-inch-long glossy black bird with a purple, bronze, and greenish cast, the common grackle has a long, keel-shaped tail, a long bill, and yellow eyes. The female is less glossy than the male.

VOICE: The male's song is a rasping *chu-seek*—like a rusty gate swinging on its hinges—uttered when the bird ruffles its feathers in display for a female. Its call is a shrill *chuck.*

BEHAVIOR: During winter and migration, these birds gather with European starlings, red-winged blackbirds, and brown-headed cowbirds in huge flocks that roost together—and they can be a nuisance to humans living nearby.

HABITAT: Cities, suburbs, farmland, pine plantations, and marshes.

NATURAL FOOD: Insects, earthworms, salamanders, and mice; the eggs and young of smaller birds; the nuts and seeds of trees, shrubs, and crops.

NEST: Most often found in colonies of 20 to 30 pairs, common grackles nest in trees, usually coniferous, as high as 60 feet above the ground. The female builds a bulky nest of grasses, debris, and sometimes mud, then lines it with grasses, feathers, and more debris; the task takes her about 11 days. The 5 pale greenish white eggs, scrawled with brown and purple, are incubated by the female for 11 or 12 days. Young can fly after about 2 weeks.

TO ATTRACT: Common grackles are unpopular with some people, but they will come for birdseed (particularly cracked corn) and suet in spring and fall.

BROWN-HEADED COWBIRD
Molothrus ater
BLACKBIRD FAMILY (ICTERIDAE)

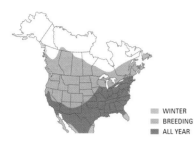

The 7-inch brown-headed cowbird male (shown at right) has a chocolate brown head, a glossy black body, and a conical bill. The female looks completely different, with mouse gray plumage and a lighter throat. Immature birds are paler than females and have heavily streaked underparts.

VOICE: The male's song is a series of high-pitched, watery, bubbly notes. The call note is *chuck*.

BEHAVIOR: In spring, a female cowbird attracts an entourage of 3 to 5 male suitors, all displaying for her and attempting to mate with her before she selects the nests into which she will lay her eggs (see below).

HABITAT: Farmland, forest edges, swamps, open fields, and suburban backyards.

NATURAL FOOD: A combination of insects, grains, and berries.

NEST: Cowbirds build no nests. Instead, the female distributes as many as 20 grayish white eggs marked with brown dots in the nests of other birds. She removes an egg from each "host" bird's nest (photo at left) and replaces it with one of her own. The host then raises the nestling cowbird—sometimes at the expense of its own young, which may be pushed out, smothered, or starved by competition from the larger cowbird chick.

TO ATTRACT: Cowbirds often show up with other blackbirds, whether you want them or not, and will eat cracked corn and millet.

BULLOCK'S AND BALTIMORE ORIOLE
Icterus bullockii, Icterus galbula
BLACKBIRD FAMILY (ICTERIDAE)

Bullock's oriole

Baltimore oriole

Previously grouped together as the northern oriole species, these handsome 8-inch birds have similar brilliant orange and black coloring. The male Baltimore oriole (right) has an entirely jet black head; the male Bullock's (left) has orange cheeks and an orange line above the eye. The Bullock's male also has more white on his black wings than the Baltimore does. Females of both species have olive-brown backs; Baltimores are burnt orange below, and Bullock's are a paler grayish yellow.

VOICE: The Baltimore oriole's song is a series of disjointed, flutelike whistles; the call is a two-part chattering *hue-lee*. The Bullock's sings a series of whistles and harsh notes and calls a harsh *cheh*.

BEHAVIOR: Male orioles arrive in their nesting territory a few days before the females and begin singing and defending it against other orioles.

HABITAT: Deciduous woodlands and forest edges, orchards, and shade trees.

NATURAL FOOD: Insects found in the trees where the birds live; also the tree fruit, including cherries and citrus.

NEST: Orioles build basketlike nests 6 to 60 feet high in elms, willows, and apple trees. The female weaves a deep pouch attached by its rim to drooping branches; it's lined with hair, wool, and fine grasses. She incubates 4 pale greenish eggs, scrawled with brown, for 12 to 14 days. Two weeks after hatching, the young are on the wing.

TO ATTRACT: Orioles will sip the juice from orange or grapefruit halves and drink sugar water from feeders. They readily visit birdbaths.

Raspberry is closer than purple to the actual hue of the 6-inch male purple finch. Most of the color is concentrated around the head, upper parts, and breast; the belly and undertail coverts are white. Females (photo at right) and young birds resemble large, heavily striped brown sparrows. Both sexes have deeply notched tails.

VOICE: The male's fast and lively warble usually repeats each note in the series. The call or alarm note is a quick *pik*.

BEHAVIOR: Purple finches spend the winter in large flocks, wandering farther south in years when food is scarce in their coniferous forest breeding grounds.

HABITAT: Coniferous forests, pine plantations, and suburban backyards with evergreens.

NATURAL FOOD: The seeds of trees and shrubs in winter, also some insects from the birds' coniferous forest home.

NEST: The female builds her nest 5 to 60 feet up on the horizontal limb of a conifer — a neat cup of twigs, grasses, and weed stems lined with fine grasses and hair. She incubates the 3 to 5 greenish spotted eggs for 13 days. Young leave in about 2 weeks.

TO ATTRACT: Sunflower seeds, in the shell and cracked, are favorites. Moving water is a lure, as are berries, fruits, and buds of deciduous trees. Conifers provide nest materials.

PURPLE FINCH
Carpodacus purpureus
FINCH FAMILY (FRINGILLIDAE)

WINTER
BREEDING
ALL YEAR

More heavily striped than the purple finch, the 6-inch male house finch (pictured) has a brownish cap but is otherwise red, orange, or yellow on head, bib, and rump. Females and juveniles are heavily streaked with brown and have less facial pattern than their purple finch counterparts. Male and female have brown, squared tails.

VOICE: The lively warbling song of both male and female is uttered in three-note phrases. The call or alarm is a sweet *queet*.

BEHAVIOR: Once restricted to the Southwest, the adaptable house finch has dramatically expanded its range since being released on Long Island in the 1940s. It is now found all across the country.

HABITAT: A great variety of habitats: deserts, open forests, farmland, and towns.

NATURAL FOOD: Seeds of trees, shrubs, and crops. The house finch is also fond of cultivated fruits and has been known to cause damage to orchards.

NEST: The female builds a cup of twigs 5 to 7 feet above the ground in a natural cavity, mailbox, building, birdhouse, or vine. She incubates the 4 or 5 sparsely dotted, pale bluish green eggs for 13 days while she's fed by the male, who regurgitates food for her. Young leave after 2 to 3 weeks.

TO ATTRACT: House finches are frequent patrons of feeders offering sunflower and thistle seeds — or birdseed mix. They consume a variety of seeds and berries from garden plants and also unopened buds of fruit trees.

HOUSE FINCH
Carpodacus mexicanus
FINCH FAMILY (FRINGILLIDAE)

WINTER
BREEDING
ALL YEAR

PINE SISKIN
Carduelis pinus
FINCH FAMILY (FRINGILLIDAE)

WINTER
BREEDING
ALL YEAR

The small, brown, heavily streaked 5-inch pine siskin has bright yellow in the wings and at the base of the tail. Male and female look alike.

VOICE: The song is a somewhat insectlike, buzzing trill that rises in pitch. The call or alarm note is *tsee-ee*.

BEHAVIOR: A shortage of tree seeds in the northern forests will send the siskins southward to search for food. Highly gregarious, they often travel with other finches in flocks of 100 birds or more, sometimes swirling into treetops like blown leaves.

HABITAT: Northern coniferous forests; also near backyard feeders.

NATURAL FOOD: Seeds from pine, spruce, fir, and other trees and shrubs; also insects, tree sap, and the nectar of tree blossoms found in their coniferous forest habitat.

NEST: Often nesting in loose colonies, the female conceals her nest of twigs, mosses, and lichens 6 to 35 feet high on a horizontal branch of a conifer. Mosses, rootlets, hair, fur, and feathers line the nest. The female lays one pale greenish blue egg per day for 3 or 4 days, beginning incubation with the first egg to reduce risk of freezing. Eggs hatch on consecutive days after 13 days of incubation. While the female incubates, the male feeds her on the nest. Young fly in about 2 weeks.

TO ATTRACT: Put out thistle seeds and sunflower seeds—and watch for large flocks to arrive. Water, alder catkins, and the conelike fruit of birch trees also appeal.

AMERICAN GOLDFINCH
Carduelis tristis
FINCH FAMILY (FRINGILLIDAE)

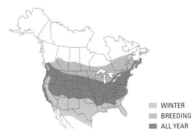

WINTER
BREEDING
ALL YEAR

In summer, the 5-inch American goldfinch male (pictured) is bright canary yellow with white wing bars and undertail coverts and a black cap, wings, and tail. The female is olive yellow with brownish black wings and tail and white wing bars (see the photo on page 84). In winter, both sexes look like the summer female, but browner.

VOICE: The male's sweet song is canarylike, rising and falling. Calls include *see-me* and the flight call *per-chick-a-ree,* uttered with each undulation.

BEHAVIOR: Gregarious most of the year, these "wild canaries" live in loose flocks of several pairs in summer, dozens and even hundreds of birds in winter.

HABITAT: Open fields, farmland, fencerows, groves, villages, and suburban backyards.

NATURAL FOOD: Seeds of thistles, dandelions, goldenrods, weeds, vegetables, and trees throughout the year; insects when available.

NEST: Nesting in late summer to coincide with maturing thistles, the female builds a tight, dense cup of vegetable fibers 4 to 14 feet high in an upright tree fork, lining it with the down of thistles and cattails. The male feeds her through the 12- to 14-day incubation of the 4 to 6 pale bluish white eggs. Both feed the offspring regurgitated, partially digested seeds for the 2 weeks they're in the nest.

TO ATTRACT: Offer water along with thistle or sunflower seeds.

The chunky, 8-inch evening grosbeak has a large, conical bill, pale in color. The male (pictured) is yellow and brown with a darker head, a yellow eye line, a short black tail, and black-and-white wings. The female is silvery cream with black and cream-colored wings. Both look flashy in flight due to their white secondary flight feathers.

VOICE: These noisy birds cheep and chirp and *clee-ip* constantly. The male's song is a lively but disjointed warble.

BEHAVIOR: In winter, these gregarious birds will fly southward in large flocks to search for food if the seeds of coniferous trees are scarce in the North.

HABITAT: Coniferous forests and mixed woodlands.

NATURAL FOOD: Primarily seeds and buds of both coniferous and deciduous trees; berries and other fruits; also insects associated with their habitat.

NEST: The female builds a fragile nest of twigs and mosses, lined with rootlets, some 20 to 60 feet high in a conifer. She incubates the 3 or 4 clear blue eggs, blotched with brown and purple, for 12 to 14 days. Young remain in the nest about 2 weeks.

TO ATTRACT: Sunflower seeds in the shell may be consumed in great quantity at stationary feeders with trays or sturdy perches. These birds also like to bathe and drink at ponds and will eat the winged pods of such deciduous trees as maples and box elders.

EVENING GROSBEAK
Coccothraustes vespertinus
FINCH FAMILY (FRINGILLIDAE)

WINTER
BREEDING
ALL YEAR

In its breeding plumage, the 6-inch male house sparrow has a gray top, chestnut nape, black bib, brown back, and gray belly. Females lack the rich chestnut coloring and the black bib, and males have less black in winter.

These birds (also called English sparrows) belong to a completely different family than native sparrows. They were introduced into North America in the mid-1800s and soon spread throughout the continent.

VOICE: A noisy, chattering bird, the house sparrow twitters and cheeps most of the time but has no real song.

BEHAVIOR: As the house sparrow made its way across the country, it displaced many native birds (such as bluebirds) from nesting sites. This gregarious bird prospers near where people live, to the extent that it's often considered a nuisance.

HABITAT: Cities, suburbs, villages, and farms.

NATURAL FOOD: Far more seeds and other vegetable matter than insects, even though house sparrows were once thought of as a potential control for destructive insects. They thrived when horses were the primary mode of transportation, ensuring abundant grain.

NEST: A pair builds its huge ball-shaped nest of grass, weeds, and trash, open on one side, inside a cavity or birdhouse, on a rafter, or behind loose boards or shutters on a building. The 5 heavily spotted white eggs are incubated by the female for 12 or 13 days, and the young leave when they are 15 to 17 days old.

TO ATTRACT: House sparrows will soon find you, especially if you provide cracked corn, red and white millet, and other seeds.

HOUSE SPARROW
Passer domesticus
OLD WORLD SPARROW FAMILY
(PASSERIDAE)

WINTER
BREEDING
ALL YEAR

TO LEARN MORE...

You can find out more about birds through the organizations and publications listed on this page. Also check bird supply stores, birding publications, bookstores, and your local library for additional useful references.

A vast amount of information is available online. Some of the most helpful websites are included in the following listings; many provide links to related websites. To find additional sites—including commercial suppliers of bird products—search under "birding," "bird feeding," "birdhouses," "binoculars," and so on.

Retail stores specializing in backyard bird supplies are on the increase. To see if there's one near you, look in the Yellow Pages under "Bird Feeders, Houses & Seed." You can also check advertisements in birding magazines for names of companies that make feeders, nest boxes, birdbaths, and other bird products.

ORGANIZATIONS

The following are sources of information about birding, bird feeding, backyard habitats, and local birding programs.

AMERICAN BIRD CONSERVANCY
PO Box 249
The Plains, VA 20198
(888)247-3624
www.abcbirds.org
Promotes conservation, publishes Bird Conservation *magazine*

AMERICAN BIRDING ASSOCIATION
PO Box 6599
Colorado Springs, CO 80934
(800)835-2473
www.americanbirding.org
Publishes birding ethics, Birding *and* North American Birds *magazines, and* Winging It *newsletters*

CORNELL UNIVERSITY LABORATORY OF ORNITHOLOGY
159 Sapsucker Woods Road
Ithaca, NY 14850
(800)843-2473
www.birds.cornell.edu (check birdsource link for bird count projects)
Sponsors Project FeederWatch and other programs, publishes Living Bird Quarterly *magazine*

NATIONAL AUDUBON SOCIETY
700 Broadway
New York, NY 10003
(212) 979-3000
www.audubon.org
Offers local chapter activities, sponsors Christmas Bird Count, publishes Audubon *magazine*

NATIONAL BIRD-FEEDING SOCIETY
PO Box 23
Northbrook, IL 60065
www.birdfeeding.org
Supports research and education about bird-feeding, publishes The Bird's-Eye reView *newsletter*

NATIONAL WILDLIFE FEDERATION
Backyard Wildlife Habitat Program
8925 Leesburg Pike
Vienna, VA 22184-0001
(703)790-4100
www.nwf.org
Supplies information on qualifying as an official wildlife habitat

NORTH AMERICAN BLUEBIRD ASSOCIATION
PO Box 74
Darlington, WI 53530
www.nabluebirdsociety.org
Provides nest box diagrams ($1 suggested donation) and information on bluebird trail

USGS PATAUXENT WILDLIFE RESEARCH CENTER
www.pwrc.usgs.gov
Offers information of general interest about birds as well as scientific research

U.S. DEPARTMENT OF AGRICULTURE NATURAL RESOURCES CONSERVATION SERVICE
7515 NE Ankeny Road
Ankeny, IA 50021
(888)526-3227
Offers "Backyard Conservation" and other publications

U.S. FISH AND WILDLIFE SERVICE DEPARTMENT OF THE INTERIOR
1849 C Street, NW
Washington, DC 20240
(703)358-1744 for refuges,
(202)208-4131 for Office of Public Affairs
www.fws.gov
Produces various publications on backyard bird habitats and a map of wildlife refuges

THE VIRTUAL BIRDER
www.virtualbirder.com
Internet birding magazine and birding simulations

FIELD GUIDES

The following are among leading North American field guides to birds. Choose a guide that is comprehensive for your region.

THE PETERSON FIELD GUIDE SERIES
Roger Tory Peterson
Houghton Mifflin Company, Boston
Regional and beginner's guides

FIELD GUIDE TO THE BIRDS OF NORTH AMERICA
Mary B. Dickinson, Editor
National Geographic Society,
Washington, DC

STOKES FIELD GUIDE TO BIRDS
Donald and Lillian Stokes
Little, Brown and Company,
Boston and New York
Eastern and western guides

FIELD GUIDE TO NORTH AMERICAN BIRDS
National Audubon Society
Alfred A. Knopf, Inc., New York
Eastern and western editions

PERIODICALS

In addition to the magazines mentioned in the previous listings, the following may be of interest as sources of information.

BIRD WATCHERS DIGEST
PO Box 110
Marietta, OH 45750-9962
(800)879-2473
www.birdwatchersdigest.com

BIRDER'S WORLD
PO Box 1612
Waukesha, WI 53187-9950
(800)533-6644
www.birdersworld.com

BIRDS & BLOOMS
PO Box 991
Greendale, WI 53129-0991
(800)344-6913
www.reimanpub.com

WILDBIRD
PO Box 52898
Boulder, CO 80322-2898
(800)365-4421

INDEX

Boldface page numbers refer to bird or plant descriptions including photos; *italic numbers* refer to photos or illustrations. In general, plants are indexed when they are prominently featured in text or photos; for plant lists, look under specific categories—annuals, grasses, perennials, and so on.

PHOTOGRAPHERS:

Academy of Natural Sciences, Philadelphia/VIREO: 68 third from top; **Walt Anderson/Visuals Unlimited, Inc.:** 63 fourth from top; **Rudolf G. Arndt/Visuals Unlimited, Inc.:** 15, 110 bottom; **Joel Arrington/Visuals Unlimited, Inc.:** 90 bottom; **Noel Barnhurst:** 41 top left, bottom left, center, bottom right; **Bill Beatty/Visuals Unlimited, Inc.:** 97 top right; **Lance Beeny:** 38 bottom right, 41 top right; **BIOS (Klein-Hubert)/Peter Arnold, Inc.:** 54 second from top; **Marion Brenner:** 54 third from top, 58 middle, 61 top; **Kathleen Norris Brenzel:** 3 top right, 18; **Gay Bumgarner:** 3 top left, 4, 7, 8 top, 10 top, 11 top, 20, 28 top right, 32 top right, 33 left, 39 right, 50 bottom right, 52 top, 60 fourth from top, 66, 67 left, middle, 107 bottom left, right, 118 top, back cover top left; **Lisa Butler:** 56 second from top; **Gary W. Carter/Visuals Unlimited, Inc.:** 104 bottom; **David Cavagnaro:** 51 top, fourth from top, 63 middle; **Peter Christiansen:** 26 bottom, 32 bottom left, 33 middle right, bottom right; **Claire Curran:** 48 top, 53 bottom right, 60 middle, 63 second from top, 71 bottom center; **R. Todd Davis:** 51 second from top; **Richard Day/Daybreak Imagery:** 1, 3 bottom left, 8 bottom, 9 top, 14, 21 bottom, 25 bottom, 29 top left, bottom right, 52 second from top, 55 bottom, 58 bottom, 59 third from top, 75 left, 77, 78 bottom, 80, 81 bottom, 84, 86 left, 88 bottom, 91 bottom right, 93 bottom, 94 top, 95 bottom, 116 bottom, 120 bottom, 124 bottom, 125 bottom; **Derrick Ditchburn/Visuals Unlimited, Inc.:** 103 bottom; **W. H. Duncan:** 68 second from top; **Tom Edwards/Visuals Unlimited, Inc.:** 22; **Derek Fell:** 57 middle, 63 top; **Todd Fink/Daybreak Imagery:** 35 bottom right, 72; **Carlyn Galati/Visuals Unlimited, Inc.:** 59 top; **Barbara Gerlach/Visuals Unlimited, Inc.:** 125 top; **Susan M. Glascock:** 55 middle, 57 bottom; **Mary Gray-Hunter:** 48 bottom; **William Grenfell/Visuals Unlimited, Inc.:** 108 left; **Pamela Harper:** 69 top center; **Lynne Harrison:** 38 top right; **Philip Harvey:** 38 bottom left; **Saxon Holt:** 12 top, 58 left; **Lynne Jackson/Visuals Unlimited, Inc.:** 97 bottom; **Arthur Lee Jacobson/Photo Garden:** 50 top center, 56 third from top; **Stephen J. Lang/Visuals Unlimited, Inc.:** 55 second from top, 88 top right; **Charles Mann:** 51 bottom, 52 third from top, 53 left, 56 top, 65 top, 69 second from top; **Sylvia Martin:** 59 second from top; **Maslowski Photo:** 2, 3 middle left, 6 left, 9 bottom, 11 bottom, 12 bottom left, right, 21 top, 24, 26 top, 32 top left, 33 right, 44, 46, 55 fourth from top, 64 second from top, 75 right, 76, 78 top left, right, 81 top right, bottom, 82, 86 bottom right, 87 bottom, 90 top right, 91 top right, 93 top, 94 bottom, 95 top, 96 top, 98, 100 top, bottom, 102 bottom, 105 bottom, 109, 113 bottom left, 114 bottom left, 115 top, 117, 118 bottom, 121 top right, 122 top left, bottom right, 123 top left, top right, back cover bottom; **S. Maslowski/Visuals Unlimited, Inc.:** 25 middle, 28 top left, bottom, 38 middle left, 42, 69 bottom, 103 top, 104 top, 106 top, 110 top, 119 top, 122 bottom left; **B. McCartney/Woodlanders, Inc.:** 68 bottom; **David McDonald:** 60 top, 61 fourth from top; **Joe McDonald/Visuals Unlimited, Inc.:** 86 top; **Mary Ann McDonald/Visuals Unlimited, Inc.:** 90 top left; **Charles W. Melton:** 53 top right, 70 top, 89 bottom, 91 left, 92, 99 bottom, 101 top, 111 top right, 114 bottom left, 121 bottom; **Jeff Milton/Daybreak Imagery:** 71 top center, back cover top right; **Terrence Moore:** 6 right; **A. & E. Morris/Birds as Art:** 100 right, 115 bottom, 122 top right; **Arthur Morris/Birds as Art:** 101 right, 102 top, 108 top right, bottom, 111 bottom right, 116 top, 118 bottom right, 124 top; **John C. Muegge/Visuals Unlimited, Inc.:** 87 top, 96 bottom, 99 top; **Jerry Pavia:** 11 right, 56 bottom, 57 top, 60 second from top, 61 middle, bottom, 64 bottom, 65 second from top; **Pamela K. Peirce:** 55 top; **Mary Carolyn Pindar:** 61 second from top; **Norman A. Plate:** 13, 23, 27, 31, 34, 35 top, 36, 37, 38 top left, 43 top right, 59 bottom, 62 left, 70 center; **Dick Poe/Visuals Unlimited, Inc.:** 83; **Sandra Lee Reha:** 10 bottom; **Rob Simpson/Visuals Unlimited, Inc.:** 113 left, top right; **Rob and Ann Simpson/Visuals Unlimited, Inc.:** 54 top, 97 top left, 101 bottom left, 105 top, 106 bottom, 107 top; **Southern Living Archive:** 65 third from top; **Joseph G. Strauch, Jr.:** 60 bottom; **Paul B. Swarmer/Visuals Unlimited, Inc.:** 123 bottom; **Michael S. Thompson:** 51 middle, 62 right, 64 top, 68 top right, 69 third from top; **Connie Toops:** 29 bottom, 39 left, 58 top; **Roger Treadwell/Visuals Unlimited, Inc.:** 25 top; **Gilbert L. Twiest/Visuals Unlimited, Inc.:** 88 left; **Tom J. Ulrich/Visuals Unlimited, Inc.:** 89 top, 112, 114 top, 120 top; **Deidra Walpole Photography:** 32 bottom left; **Gary Walter/Visuals Unlimited, Inc.:** 67 top right; **William J. Weber/Visuals Unlimited, Inc.:** 119 bottom; **Peter Whiteley:** 35 bottom; **Tom Woodward:** 49, 50 left, 52 bottom, 54 bottom, 63 bottom, 65 right, 68 left, 69 right, 71 top left, right, bottom left; **Tom Wyatt:** 43 top left, top center, bottom, 64 third from top.